SHIMBA
BIBLE STUDY SERIES

THE DIVINITY OF JESUS

IN THE BOOK OF REVELATION

Dr. Maxwell Shimba

TABLE OF CONTENTS

TABLE OF CONTENTS

INTRODUCTION

The Book of Revelation, the final book of the New Testament, stands as one of the most profound and enigmatic texts in Christian scripture. Penned by the Apostle John during his exile on the island of Patmos, this apocalyptic vision reveals the ultimate triumph of Jesus Christ over the forces of evil. It is within these pages that we encounter the most vivid and awe-inspiring depictions of Jesus' divinity, sovereignty, and eternal reign. As we delve into The Divinity of Jesus in the Book of Revelation, we aim to uncover the rich theological truths and the vital lessons that these revelations impart to believers.

Revelation is a book replete with symbolism, prophecy, and vivid imagery, portraying the cosmic struggle between good and evil, and the ultimate victory of Christ. This work aims to provide a comprehensive understanding of Jesus' divine nature as revealed in Revelation, exploring how He is depicted as the Alpha and Omega, the faithful witness, the firstborn from the dead, and the ruler over the kings of the earth. Each of these titles and depictions serves to affirm His supreme authority and eternal sovereignty.

The Apostle John's visions in Revelation offer a unique perspective on the nature of Jesus Christ, highlighting His roles as both the sacrificial Lamb and the conquering King. From the initial vision of the glorified Christ in Revelation 1, where He stands among the seven golden lampstands, to the climactic scenes of His return and the establishment of the new heaven and new earth, each chapter of Revelation unveils different aspects of Jesus' divinity. This introduction will set the stage for a deeper exploration of these themes, providing the necessary context and framework for understanding the intricate details of the subsequent chapters.

One of the central themes in Revelation is the sovereignty of Jesus Christ over all creation. He is described as the Alpha and the Omega, the beginning and the end, signifying His eternal nature and unchanging authority. This title, unique to the Book of Revelation, encapsulates the totality of Jesus' divine essence, affirming that He is the source and the culmination of all things. The declaration of Jesus as the Alpha and Omega is a powerful reminder of His eternal presence and His ultimate control over the unfolding of history.

Another key aspect of Jesus' divinity in Revelation is His role as the righteous judge. Throughout the visions, Jesus is depicted as the one who holds the keys to death and Hades, who opens the scroll and its seven seals, and who ultimately judges the living and the dead. His judgments are portrayed as true and just, reflecting His holiness and righteousness. These depictions challenge believers to recognize the seriousness of divine judgment and the importance of living in accordance with God's will.

The Book of Revelation also provides a profound glimpse into the ultimate destiny of believers and the eternal kingdom of God. The visions of the new heaven and new earth, the New Jerusalem, and the river of life paint a picture of the perfect and eternal reign of Jesus Christ. These visions offer hope and encouragement, assuring believers of the fulfillment of God's promises and the ultimate restoration of all things. The descriptions of eternal life and the eradication of pain, sorrow, and death underscore the completeness of Jesus' redemptive work and His divine authority to bring about this transformation.

In The Divinity of Jesus in the Book of Revelation, we will embark on a detailed expository study of the key passages and themes that highlight Jesus' divine nature. Using exhaustive references to Strong's Concordance, we will delve into the original Greek terms and their meanings, providing a richer and more nuanced understanding of the text. Through this study, we aim to deepen our appreciation of the theological depth and the spiritual significance of Jesus' divinity as revealed in the Book of Revelation. This introduction serves as the foundation for the journey ahead, inviting readers to explore the profound mysteries and the glorious truths of Jesus Christ as the divine and eternal King.

DR. MAXWELL SHIMBA

CHAPTER 01

THE CONTEXT OF REVELATION

The Book of Revelation, also known as the Apocalypse, is the final book of the New Testament. It is a profound and intricate work, attributed to the Apostle John. John wrote this book while he was in exile on the island of Patmos, likely around AD 95-96, during the reign of the Roman Emperor Domitian. This context is essential, as it was a time of severe persecution for Christians. The imagery and symbolism of Revelation would have provided both comfort and hope to its original audience, assuring them of Christ's ultimate victory over evil.

The Purpose of Revelation

Revelation serves multiple purposes. It is both a prophetic and an apocalyptic text, revealing future events and the ultimate triumph of good over evil. It also serves as a pastoral letter to the seven churches in Asia Minor, offering guidance, encouragement, and warnings. The primary purpose of Revelation, however, is to reveal Jesus Christ in His glory, power, and authority.

Jesus, the Alpha and Omega

In Revelation, Jesus is referred to as the Alpha and Omega, the first and last letters of the Greek alphabet. This title emphasizes His eternal nature and supreme authority over all creation. Revelation 1:8 states, "I am the Alpha and the Omega, says the Lord God, who is and who was and who is to come, the Almighty." This verse establishes Jesus as eternal, existing beyond the confines of time.

In Revelation 22:13, Jesus reiterates this truth: "I am the Alpha and the Omega, the First and the Last, the Beginning and the End." This declaration not only underscores His divinity but also His role as the Creator and Consummator of all things. By identifying Himself with these titles, Jesus asserts His sovereignty over history and His ultimate authority in the divine plan of salvation.

The Vision of Christ

John's initial vision of Christ sets the tone for the entire book. In Revelation 1:12-16, John describes seeing Jesus in a glorified state:

> "Then I turned to see the voice that was speaking to me, and on turning I saw seven golden lampstands, and in the midst of the lampstands one like a son of man, clothed with a long robe and with a golden sash around his chest. The hairs of his head were white, like white wool, like snow. His

eyes were like a flame of fire, his feet were like burnished bronze, refined in a furnace, and his voice was like the roar of many waters. In his right hand he held seven stars, from his mouth came a sharp two-edged sword, and his face was like the sun shining in full strength."

This vision is rich with symbolism. The seven golden lampstands represent the seven churches (Revelation 1:20), indicating Christ's presence among His people. The white hair signifies His purity and eternal wisdom, while the eyes of fire symbolize His penetrating vision and judgment. The feet of burnished bronze denote His strength and stability, and the voice like many waters reflects His powerful and authoritative proclamation. The sharp two-edged sword coming from His mouth represents the Word of God, which is living and active (Hebrews 4:12). Finally, His face shining like the sun emphasizes His divine glory.

The Letters to the Seven Churches

Chapters 2 and 3 of Revelation contain letters to the seven churches in Asia Minor: Ephesus, Smyrna, Pergamum, Thyatira, Sardis, Philadelphia, and Laodicea. Each letter includes a specific message from Christ, tailored to the unique circumstances and challenges faced by each congregation. These letters provide valuable lessons for believers today, as they address issues such as love, faithfulness, repentance, perseverance, and spiritual vigilance.

Ephesus: The Call to Return to First Love

To the church in Ephesus, Jesus says, "I know your deeds, your hard work and your perseverance. I know that you cannot tolerate wicked people, that you have tested those who claim to be apostles but are not, and have found them false. You have persevered and have endured hardships for my name, and have not grown weary. Yet I hold this against you: You have forsaken the love you had at first" (Revelation 2:2-4).

Jesus commends the Ephesians for their diligence and discernment but rebukes them for abandoning their first love. He calls them to remember, repent, and return to their initial passion for Him. This message underscores the importance of maintaining a vibrant, loving relationship with Christ.

Smyrna: Faithfulness unto Death

To the church in Smyrna, Jesus offers words of encouragement: "Do not be afraid of what you are about to suffer. I tell you, the devil will put some of you in prison to test you, and you will suffer persecution for ten days. Be faithful, even to the point of death, and I will give you life as your victor's crown" (Revelation 2:10).

Jesus acknowledges the suffering of the Smyrnan believers and exhorts them to remain faithful, even unto death. He promises the crown of life to those who endure, highlighting the eternal rewards for steadfast faith in the face of persecution.

Pergamum: Holding Fast Despite Opposition

To the church in Pergamum, Jesus says, "I know where you live—where Satan has his throne. Yet you remain true to my name. You did not renounce your faith in me, not even in the days of Antipas, my faithful witness, who was put to death in your city—where Satan lives" (Revelation 2:13).

Despite living in a place of intense spiritual opposition, the believers in Pergamum hold fast to their faith. However, Jesus warns them against tolerating false teachings and calls for repentance. This message emphasizes the need for doctrinal purity and perseverance in the truth.

Thyatira: Rejecting Immorality and False Teaching

To the church in Thyatira, Jesus says, "I know your deeds, your love and faith, your service and perseverance, and that you are now doing more than you did at first. Nevertheless, I have this against you: You tolerate that woman Jezebel, who calls herself a prophet. By her teaching she misleads my servants into sexual immorality and the eating of food sacrificed to idols" (Revelation 2:19-20).

Jesus commends the Thyatirans for their growth in love and service but rebukes them for tolerating false teaching and immorality. He calls for repentance and warns of severe consequences for those who do not turn away from such practices. This letter highlights the importance of moral integrity and rejecting false prophets.

Sardis: A Call to Wake Up

To the church in Sardis, Jesus says, "I know your deeds; you have a reputation of being alive, but you are dead. Wake up! Strengthen what remains and is about to die, for I have found your deeds unfinished in the sight of my God" (Revelation 3:1-2).

Jesus calls the Sardians to wake up and strengthen their spiritual lives. He warns them to remember what they have received and heard, to obey it, and to repent. This message emphasizes the need for spiritual vigilance and renewal.

Philadelphia: An Open Door

To the church in Philadelphia, Jesus says, "I know your deeds. See, I have placed before you an open door that no one can shut. I know that you have little strength, yet you have kept my word and have not denied my name" (Revelation 3:8).

Jesus commends the Philadelphians for their faithfulness and promises them an open door of opportunity and protection. He assures them of His love and the ultimate victory over their enemies. This letter highlights the rewards of steadfast faith and obedience.

Laodicea: A Call to Zeal

To the church in Laodicea, Jesus says, "I know your deeds, that you are neither cold nor hot. I wish you were either one or the other! So, because you are lukewarm—neither hot nor cold—I am about to spit you out of my mouth" (Revelation 3:15-16).

Jesus rebukes the Laodiceans for their lukewarm faith and complacency. He calls them to repent and be zealous, offering the promise of intimate fellowship with Him. This message underscores the danger of spiritual complacency and the need for wholehearted commitment to Christ.

The Expository Approach

An expository study of Revelation involves examining the text closely, and considering its historical context, literary structure, and theological significance. Using exhaustive Strong's Concordance, we can delve deeper into the meanings of key terms and phrases.

For instance, the term "Alpha and Omega" (Strong's G1 and G5598) signifies the completeness and eternal nature of Christ. "Alpha" is the first letter of the Greek alphabet, and "Omega" is the last, symbolizing that Jesus encompasses all things from beginning to end.

Conclusion

The Book of Revelation provides a profound and multifaceted revelation of Jesus Christ. As the Alpha and Omega, He is eternal and sovereign, holding ultimate authority over all creation. The messages to the seven churches offer timeless lessons for believers, calling us to faithfulness, repentance, and steadfastness in the face of trials. By studying Revelation expositively and considering the deeper meanings of its key terms, we can gain a richer understanding of Christ's divine attributes and His ultimate victory over evil.

CHAPTER 02

JESUS, THE ALPHA AND OMEGA

The Book of Revelation offers a profound revelation of Jesus Christ, not only as the Lamb of God but also as the Alpha and Omega, the beginning and the end. This title underscores His eternal existence, His sovereign authority, and His ultimate role in the divine plan of creation and redemption. In this chapter, we will explore the significance of Jesus as the Alpha and Omega, using biblical references and an expository study with exhaustive Strong's Concordance to delve deeper into this divine attribute.

Jesus Declares His Eternal Nature

In Revelation 1:8, Jesus declares, "I am the Alpha and the Omega, the Beginning and the End, who is and who was and who is to come, the Almighty." This declaration is a powerful affirmation of His eternal nature and omnipotence.

The terms "Alpha" and "Omega" are the first and last letters of the Greek alphabet, symbolizing that Jesus is the beginning and the end of all things.

- Alpha (ἄλφα - Strong's G1): The first letter of the Greek alphabet, representing the beginning.

- Omega (ὤ - Strong's G5598): The last letter of the Greek alphabet, representing the end.

By identifying Himself as both Alpha and Omega, Jesus emphasizes His eternal presence and His role in the entirety of creation. He is the origin (beginning) and the culmination (end) of all existence.

The Beginning and the End

In Revelation 22:13, Jesus reiterates this truth: "I am the Alpha and the Omega, the First and the Last, the Beginning and the End." This declaration further emphasizes His eternal nature and His supreme authority over time and creation.

- First (πρῶτος - Strong's G4413): Denotes primacy and preeminence.

- Last (ἔσχατος - Strong's G2078): Denotes the finality and conclusion.

This duality signifies that Jesus is not only present at the creation of the universe but also at its consummation. He is the eternal, self-existent one who encompasses all time and space.

The Eternal and Omnipotent Christ

Revelation 1:17-18 provides another profound glimpse into Jesus' divine nature. John writes, "When I saw him, I fell at his feet as though dead. But he laid his right hand on me, saying, 'Fear not, I am the first and the last, and the living one. I died, and behold I am alive forevermore, and I have the keys of Death and Hades.'"

- First (πρῶτος - Strong's G4413) and Last (ἔσχατος - Strong's G2078): Reinforces Jesus' eternal existence.

- Living One (ζῶν - Strong's G2198): Emphasizes that Jesus is alive forevermore, having conquered death.

Jesus' statement that He holds "the keys of Death and Hades" signifies His ultimate authority over life and death. This authority is rooted in His eternal nature and His victory over death through His resurrection.

Jesus in the Context of Revelation

The Book of Revelation portrays Jesus in various roles, each reinforcing His identity as the Alpha and Omega:

1. The Glorified Christ (Revelation 1:12-16): In this vision, Jesus is depicted with eyes like a flame of fire, feet like burnished bronze, and a voice like the roar of many waters. These symbols emphasize His divine majesty and authority.

2. The Lamb of God (Revelation 5:6-14): Jesus is depicted as the Lamb who was slain, worthy to open the scroll and execute God's plan. This role highlights His sacrificial love and redemptive power.

3. The Victorious Warrior (Revelation 19:11-16): Jesus is depicted as a rider on a white horse, leading the armies of heaven. This imagery underscores His ultimate victory over evil and His role as the righteous judge.

4. The Bridegroom (Revelation 21:2): Jesus is presented as the Bridegroom who welcomes His bride, the church, into the new heaven and new earth. This role highlights His loving and eternal relationship with His people.

Theological Implications

The title "Alpha and Omega" has profound theological implications. It affirms several key aspects of Jesus' identity:

1. Eternal Existence: Jesus exists beyond the confines of time. He is the eternal "I AM" (Exodus 3:14), existing before the creation of the world and continuing forever.

2. Sovereign Authority: Jesus has ultimate authority over all creation. As the Alpha and Omega, He controls the beginning and the end, and everything in between.

3. Redemptive Power: Jesus' death and resurrection are central to His identity as the Alpha and Omega. He is the

living one who conquered death, providing redemption and eternal life to all who believe.

4. Cosmic Role: Jesus' role extends beyond the church to encompass the entire cosmos. He is the Lord of all creation, and His ultimate victory will restore and renew the heavens and the earth.

Conclusion

In the Book of Revelation, Jesus' declarations as the Alpha and Omega reveal His divine nature and eternal sovereignty. Through His roles as the Glorified Christ, the Lamb of God, the Victorious Warrior, and the Bridegroom, Jesus demonstrates His authority, power, and love. By understanding these aspects of His identity, believers can find assurance in His eternal presence and His ultimate victory over evil. As the Alpha and Omega, Jesus is the source and conclusion of all creation, holding the keys to life, death, and everything beyond. This profound truth offers hope and encouragement, reminding us that in Jesus, we have an eternal and unshakable foundation.

Jesus, the Alpha and Omega

In Revelation 1:4-8, we encounter an extended greeting that introduces the core themes of the Book of Revelation. These verses set the stage by addressing the seven churches in Asia Minor and emphasizing the divine origin and authority of the message. John, the human author, emphasizes that the true authors are God the Father, Jesus Christ, and the Holy Spirit, referred to as the "seven Spirits who are before His throne." This chapter will delve into the profound declaration of Jesus as the Alpha and Omega, exploring its significance through a detailed expository study using exhaustive Strong's Concordance and other biblical references.

The Greetings to the Seven Churches

Revelation 1:4-5 begins with a greeting from John to the seven churches in Asia Minor: "John, to the seven churches which are in Asia: Grace to you and peace from Him who is and who was and who is to come, and from the seven Spirits who are before His throne, and from Jesus Christ, the faithful witness, the firstborn from the dead, and the ruler over the kings of the earth."

This greeting is rich with theological significance, highlighting the eternal nature of God the Father, the role of the Holy Spirit, and the exalted position of Jesus Christ.

- Him who is and who was and who is to come: This phrase underscores God's eternal nature and His sovereignty over past, present, and future. It is reminiscent of God's self-revelation as "I AM" in Exodus 3:14.

- Seven Spirits: The "seven Spirits who are before His throne" is a complex and often debated phrase. It likely symbolizes the fullness and perfection of the Holy Spirit, echoing the sevenfold Spirit described in Isaiah 11:2.

- Jesus Christ: Jesus is introduced with three significant titles:

- Faithful Witness (μάρτυς - Strong's G3144): This emphasizes Jesus' role in revealing God's truth.

- Firstborn from the Dead (πρωτότοκος - Strong's G4416): This signifies Jesus' preeminence in resurrection, indicating that He is the first to rise from the dead, never to die again.

- Ruler over the Kings of the Earth (ἄρχων - Strong's G758): This denotes His supreme authority over all earthly rulers, affirming His kingship.

Jesus' Love and Sacrifice

Revelation 1:5-6 continues, "To Him who loved us and washed us from our sins in His own blood, and has made us kings and priests to His God and Father, to Him be glory and dominion forever and ever. Amen."

These verses highlight Jesus' redemptive work and His love for humanity:

- Loved us (ἀγαπάω - Strong's G25): This speaks to the profound, sacrificial love of Jesus.

- Washed us from our sins (λυ□ω - Strong's G3089): The term "washed" indicates a thorough cleansing from sin, accomplished by Jesus' sacrificial death.

- Kings and priests (βασιλευ□ς - Strong's G935, ἱερεύς - Strong's G2409): This denotes the elevated status believers receive through Jesus, sharing in His royal and priestly roles.

The Declaration of Jesus' Return

Revelation 1:7 proclaims, "Behold, He is coming with clouds, and every eye will see Him, even they who pierced Him. And all the tribes of the earth will mourn because of Him. Even so, Amen."

This verse serves as a prophetic declaration of Jesus' second coming:

- Coming with clouds (ἔ□ρχομαι - Strong's G2064): This imagery is associated with divine presence and glory, as seen in Daniel 7:13 and Matthew 24:30.

- Every eye will see Him: This emphasizes the universal visibility and impact of Jesus' return.

- Mourn (κο□πτω - Strong's G2875): The mourning of the tribes signifies the recognition of Jesus' true identity and the reality of judgment for those who rejected Him.

Jesus, the Alpha and Omega

Revelation 1:8 provides a climactic affirmation of Jesus' divine identity: "'I am the Alpha and the Omega, the

Beginning and the End,' says the Lord, 'who is and who was and who is to come, the Almighty.'"

- Alpha (α λφα - Strong's G1) and Omega (Ωμέγα - Strong's G5598): These letters, the first and last of the Greek alphabet, symbolize completeness and eternity.

- Beginning (ἀρχή - Strong's G746) and End (τέλος - Strong's G5056): These terms reinforce Jesus as the origin and conclusion of all things, echoing His role in creation (John 1:1-3) and His consummation of history (Revelation 21:6).

- The Almighty (παντοκρα τωρ - Strong's G3841): This title emphasizes Jesus' omnipotence, equating Him with the sovereign God of the Old Testament (Isaiah 44:6; 41:4).

Old Testament Fulfillment

John's identification of Jesus as the Alpha and Omega draws heavily on Old Testament themes and prophecies. Isaiah 44:6 and 41:4 declare God as the first and the last, asserting His exclusive divinity and eternal existence. By applying these titles to Jesus, John affirms His divine nature and continuity with Yahweh, the God of Israel.

Isaiah 46:10 further emphasizes God's sovereignty in declaring "the end from the beginning," highlighting His control over history and His ability to fulfill His purposes. This background enriches our understanding of Jesus as the

Alpha and Omega, the one who orchestrates and consummates God's redemptive plan.

The Seven Spirits

The greeting in Revelation 1:4 includes "from the seven Spirits who are before His throne." This phrase has been interpreted in various ways:

1. Angelic: Some view the seven Spirits as angelic beings, but this interpretation lacks strong biblical support.

2. Symbolic: Others see it as a symbol of completeness and perfection, aligning with the frequent symbolic use of the number seven in Revelation.

3. Mystical: A mystical interpretation considers it a reference to divine attributes or activities.

4. Trinitarian: The most widely accepted view among Catholics and Protestants is Trinitarian, identifying the seven Spirits with the Holy Spirit, drawing from Isaiah 11:2's sevenfold description of the Spirit of the Lord.

Revelation 5:6 associates the seven Spirits with the Lamb's seven eyes, "which are the seven Spirits of God sent out into all the earth." This imagery likely alludes to Zechariah 3:9 and 4:10, where the seven eyes of the Lord represent divine omniscience and presence throughout the earth.

Conclusion

The greeting in Revelation 1:4-8 serves as a powerful introduction to the themes of the book, emphasizing the divine authority and eternal nature of Jesus Christ. As the Alpha and Omega, Jesus encompasses the entirety of existence, from creation to consummation. His declarations in these verses affirm His divinity, sovereignty, and ultimate victory over all things.

Through an expository study using exhaustive Strong's Concordance, we gain deeper insight into the significance of these titles and their Old Testament background. Understanding Jesus as the Alpha and Omega enriches our comprehension of His role in God's redemptive plan and assures us of His eternal presence and ultimate authority. As we continue to explore the Book of Revelation, these foundational truths will provide a framework for interpreting its profound and complex visions.

CHAPTER 03

LESSONS FROM THE SEVEN CHURCHES – EPHESUS

In Revelation 2:1-7, Jesus addresses the church in Ephesus, the first of the seven churches in Asia Minor. This message is both commendatory and corrective, providing valuable lessons for believers about maintaining their first love for Christ. By examining these verses through an expository study with exhaustive Strong's Concordance, we can gain a deeper understanding of the spiritual state of the Ephesian church and the timeless lessons Jesus imparts.

The Commendation

Jesus begins His message to the Ephesian church with words of commendation. Revelation 2:1-3 states:

> "To the angel of the church of Ephesus write, 'These things says He who holds the seven stars in His right hand, who walks in the midst of the seven golden lampstands: 'I know your works, your labor, your patience, and that you cannot bear those who are evil. And you have tested those who say they are apostles and are not, and have found them liars; and you have persevered and have patience, and have labored for My name's sake and have not become weary.'"

- Seven Stars (α□ γγελος - Strong's G32): Refers to the angels or messengers of the seven churches, symbolizing their leaders.

- Seven Golden Lampstands (λυ□ χνος - Strong's G3087): Represent the seven churches (Revelation 1:20).

Jesus, who holds the seven stars and walks among the lampstands, signifies His authority over and presence within the churches. He acknowledges the hard work, perseverance, and discernment of the Ephesian believers:

- Works (ε□ ργον - Strong's G2041): Refers to their deeds and actions in serving Christ.

- Labor (κο□ πος - Strong's G2873): Emphasizes the strenuous effort and toil in their ministry.

- Patience (ὑπομονή - Strong's G5281): Highlights their endurance and steadfastness in the face of trials.

The Ephesians are commended for their intolerance of evil and their discernment in identifying false apostles. Their perseverance and endurance for Jesus' name's sake are notable, as they have not grown weary in their faith and service.

The Correction

Despite the commendation, Jesus has a significant correction for the Ephesian church. Revelation 2:4-5 states:

> "Nevertheless I have this against you, that you have left your first love. Remember therefore from where you have fallen; repent and do the first works, or else I will come to you quickly and remove your lampstand from its place—unless you repent."

- Left (ἀφίημι - Strong's G863): Indicates abandoning or neglecting.

- First Love (ἀγάπη - Strong's G26): Refers to the initial fervent love for Christ and for one another.

Jesus points out that the Ephesian church has left its first love. This love, characterized by fervent devotion and passion for Christ, has waned. Despite their commendable deeds, they have lost the essence of their initial relationship with Jesus.

The Call to Remember and Repent

Jesus provides a threefold remedy for the Ephesians' condition: remember, repent, and return to the first works.

- Remember (μνημονευ□ω - Strong's G3421): Calls the believers to recall their initial state of fervent love and devotion.

- Repent (μετανοε□ω - Strong's G3340): Involves a change of mind and heart, turning away from their current state and returning to their first love.

- First Works (πρῶτος - Strong's G4413): Refers to the deeds and actions motivated by their initial love for Christ.

Jesus warns that if they do not repent, He will remove their lampstand from its place, symbolizing the removal of their status as a church. This highlights the seriousness of their condition and the urgent need for repentance.

The Promise to Overcomers

Revelation 2:6-7 concludes the message with an additional commendation and a promise:

> "But this you have, that you hate the deeds of the Nicolaitans, which I also hate. He who has an ear, let him hear what the Spirit says to the churches. To him who overcomes I will give to eat from the tree of life, which is in the midst of the Paradise of God."

- Nicolaitans (Νικολαϊ□της - Strong's G3531): A sect whose deeds and teachings were detestable to Christ. Their exact identity is uncertain, but they likely promoted moral and doctrinal compromise.

- Tree of Life (ξύλον - Strong's G3586): Symbolizes eternal life, first mentioned in Genesis 2:9 and 3:22-24, and reappearing in Revelation 22:2, 14, 19.

- Paradise (παρα□δεισος - Strong's G3857): Refers to the blissful abode of the righteous, often associated with the Garden of Eden and heaven.

Jesus commends the Ephesians for hating the deeds of the Nicolaitans, aligning their stance with His. He then offers a promise to the overcomers—those who heed His message and overcome their shortcomings. They will have the privilege of eating from the tree of life in the Paradise of God, signifying the restoration of eternal life and fellowship with God.

Expository Insights

Examining the text through exhaustive Strong's Concordance reveals deeper meanings and connections:

- α□γγελος (Strong's G32): While often translated as "angel," it can also mean "messenger," implying the leaders of the churches.

- λυ□χνος (Strong's G3087): The lampstands symbolize the churches, reflecting their role as light-bearers in the world (Matthew 5:14-16).

- ε□ργον (Strong's G2041): Emphasizes the tangible actions and ministries carried out by the church.

- κο□πος (Strong's G2873): Denotes laborious effort, underscoring the Ephesians' dedication.

- ὑπομονή (Strong's G5281): Patience or endurance, a crucial virtue in the face of persecution and trials.

- ἀφίημι (Strong's G863): The act of leaving or forsaking, indicating a deliberate departure from their initial love.

- ἀγάπη (Strong's G26): The highest form of love, selfless and sacrificial, exemplified by Christ.

- μετανοε□ω (Strong's G3340): True repentance involves a transformative change in direction and behavior.

Practical Application

The message to the church in Ephesus holds timeless relevance for believers today. Key lessons include:

1. Maintain First Love: Our relationship with Christ should be characterized by fervent love and devotion. Acts of service and doctrinal correctness must flow from a genuine love for Jesus.

2. Discernment and Purity: Like the Ephesians, we must exercise discernment and reject false teachings and immoral practices. Maintaining purity in doctrine and life is essential.

3. Repentance and Renewal: When our love for Christ wanes, we must remember our initial devotion, repent, and return to the deeds motivated by that love. True repentance brings restoration and renewal.

4. Promise to Overcomers: Jesus offers eternal rewards to those who overcome spiritual complacency and compromise. Our faithfulness will be rewarded with eternal life and fellowship with God.

Conclusion

The message to the church in Ephesus in Revelation 2:1-7 provides a profound lesson on the importance of maintaining our first love for Christ. Through commendation, correction, and promise, Jesus calls believers to a fervent and enduring relationship with Him. By examining these verses through an expository study with exhaustive Strong's Concordance, we uncover the depth of Jesus' message and its enduring relevance for the church today. As we heed His call to remember, repent, and return to our first love, we will experience the fullness of His presence and the eternal rewards He promises to those who overcome.

Lessons from the Seven Churches - Smyrna

In Revelation 2:8-11, Jesus addresses the church in Smyrna, the second of the seven churches in Asia Minor. This message is one of encouragement and exhortation, focusing on faithfulness in the face of persecution. By examining these verses through an expository study with exhaustive Strong's Concordance, we can uncover the deeper meanings and timeless lessons Jesus imparts to the believers in Smyrna and to Christians today.

The Greeting

Jesus begins His message to the church in Smyrna with a greeting that emphasizes His eternal nature and victory over death. Revelation 2:8 states:

> "And to the angel of the church in Smyrna write, 'These things says the First and the Last, who was dead, and came to life.'"

- Angel (ἄγγελος - Strong's G32): Refers to the messenger or leader of the church.

- First (πρῶτος - Strong's G4413) and Last (ἔσχατος - Strong's G2078): These titles emphasize Jesus' eternal existence and sovereignty over all things.

- Was Dead (νεκρός - Strong's G3498) and Came to Life (ζάω - Strong's G2198): This highlights Jesus' victory over death through His resurrection, offering hope to those facing persecution.

By identifying Himself as the First and the Last, Jesus assures the Smyrnan believers of His eternal presence and sovereignty. His victory over death serves as a powerful reminder that He has the ultimate authority over life and death.

The Commendation

Jesus continues His message with words of commendation for the church in Smyrna. Revelation 2:9 states:

> "I know your works, tribulation, and poverty (but you are rich); and I know the blasphemy of those who say they are Jews and are not, but are a synagogue of Satan."

- Works (ε ργον - Strong's G2041): Refers to the deeds and actions of the believers.

- Tribulation (θλῖψις - Strong's G2347): Signifies the suffering and persecution they endure.

- Poverty (πτωχει α - Strong's G4432): Indicates their material lack, contrasting with their spiritual richness.

- Blasphemy (βλασφημι α - Strong's G988): Refers to the slander and false accusations from those who claim to be Jews but are not truly following God.

- Synagogue of Satan (Συναγωγη τοῦ Σατανᾶ - Strong's G4864 & G4567): This harsh term indicates the opposition from false Jews who are acting under satanic influence.

Jesus acknowledges the works, tribulation, and poverty of the Smyrnan church, affirming their spiritual richness despite their material lack. He also recognizes the blasphemy and opposition they face from those who falsely claim to be Jews. This commendation emphasizes the faithfulness and resilience of the Smyrnan believers in the midst of severe trials.

The Exhortation

Revelation 2:10 provides an exhortation and a promise to the believers in Smyrna:

> "Do not fear any of those things which you are about to suffer. Indeed, the devil is about to throw some of you into prison, that you may be tested, and you will have tribulation ten days. Be faithful until death, and I will give you the crown of life."

- Fear (φοβε□ω - Strong's G5399): Jesus commands them not to fear the impending suffering.

- Devil (δια□βολος - Strong's G1228): Indicates the ultimate source of their persecution.

- Tested (πειρα□ζω - Strong's G3985): Refers to the trials and challenges designed to test their faith.

- Ten Days (δε□κα ἡμέραι - Strong's G1176 & G2250): This symbolic period suggests a limited time of intense persecution.

- Faithful (πιστο□ς - Strong's G4103): Emphasizes steadfastness and loyalty to Christ.

- Crown of Life (στε□ φανος - Strong's G4735 & ζωη□ - Strong's G2222): Represents the eternal reward for those who remain faithful, symbolizing victory and eternal life.

Jesus' exhortation calls the Smyrnan believers to remain fearless and faithful in the face of impending persecution. He assures them that their suffering, though intense, will be limited in duration. The promise of the crown of life serves as an encouragement to persevere, offering the hope of eternal reward and victory.

The Promise to Overcomers

Revelation 2:11 concludes the message with a promise to the overcomers:

> "He who has an ear, let him hear what the Spirit says to the churches. He who overcomes shall not be hurt by the second death."

- He who has an ear (ὁ ε□ χων ους - Strong's G2192 & G3775): A call to attentive listening and understanding.

- Overcomes (νικα□ ω - Strong's G3528): Refers to those who remain faithful and victorious in their faith.

- Second Death (δευ□ τερος θα□ νατος - Strong's G1208 & G2288): Symbolizes eternal separation from God, as described in Revelation 20:14 and 21:8.

The promise to overcomers assures the Smyrnan believers that those who remain faithful will not be hurt by the second death. This promise emphasizes the ultimate victory and eternal security of those who persevere in their faith, even unto death.

Expository Insights

Examining the text through exhaustive Strong's Concordance reveals deeper meanings and connections:

- ἄγγελος (Strong's G32): While often translated as "angel," it can also mean "messenger," implying the leaders of the churches.

- πρῶτος (Strong's G4413) and ἔσχατος (Strong's G2078): These titles affirm Jesus' eternal existence and sovereignty.

- νεκρός (Strong's G3498) and ζάω (Strong's G2198): Highlight Jesus' victory over death and His eternal life.

- ἔργον (Strong's G2041): Emphasizes the tangible actions and ministries carried out by the church.

- θλῖψις (Strong's G2347): Signifies the intense suffering and persecution faced by the believers.

- πτωχεία (Strong's G4432): Indicates material poverty, contrasted with spiritual richness.

- βλασφημία (Strong's G988): Refers to slander and false accusations from opponents.

- Συναγωγη□ του̃ Σατανα̃ (Strong's G4864 & G4567): Indicates the opposition from false Jews under satanic influence.

- πειρα□ ζω (Strong's G3985): Refers to testing and trials designed to prove the believers' faith.

- στε□ φανος (Strong's G4735) & ζωη□ (Strong's G2222): Represent the crown of life, symbolizing victory and eternal reward.

- νικα□ ω (Strong's G3528): Refers to overcoming and remaining victorious in faith.

- δευ□ τερος θα□ νατος (Strong's G1208 & G2288): Symbolizes eternal separation from God, highlighting the ultimate consequence for the unfaithful.

Practical Application

The message to the church in Smyrna holds timeless relevance for believers today. Key lessons include:

1. Faithfulness in Persecution: Believers are called to remain faithful and fearless in the face of trials and persecution. Our steadfastness is rooted in the assurance of Christ's victory over death.

2. Spiritual Richness: True wealth is found in spiritual richness, not material abundance. Even in poverty and tribulation, believers can possess great spiritual wealth.

3. Hope of Eternal Reward: The promise of the crown of life and victory over the second death provides hope and encouragement to persevere in faith. Our eternal reward far surpasses any temporal suffering.

4. Discernment and Resilience: Recognizing and rejecting false teachings and opposition is crucial. Believers must remain discerning and resilient in their faith.

Conclusion

The message to the church in Smyrna in Revelation 2:8-11 provides a profound lesson on faithfulness in the face of persecution. Through commendation, exhortation, and promise, Jesus calls believers to remain steadfast and fearless, holding onto the hope of eternal reward. By examining these verses through an expository study with exhaustive Strong's Concordance, we uncover the depth of Jesus' message and its enduring relevance for the church today. As we heed His call to faithfulness, we will experience the fullness of His presence and the eternal rewards He promises to those who overcome.

Lessons from the Seven Churches - Pergamum

In Revelation 2:12-17, Jesus addresses the church in Pergamum, the third of the seven churches in Asia Minor. This message emphasizes the importance of holding fast to faith despite external pressures and the dangers of compromising with false teachings. By examining these verses through an expository study with exhaustive Strong's Concordance, we can uncover the deeper meanings and timeless lessons Jesus imparts to the believers in Pergamum and to Christians today.

The Greeting

Jesus begins His message to the church in Pergamum with a greeting that underscores His authority and judgment. Revelation 2:12 states:

> "And to the angel of the church in Pergamum write, 'These things says He who has the sharp two-edged sword.'"

- Angel (α□γγελος - Strong's G32): Refers to the messenger or leader of the church.

- Sharp Two-edged Sword (ρομφαία δίστομος οξεῖα - Strong's G4501, G1366, G3691): Symbolizes the Word of God and Christ's authority to judge and discern truth from falsehood (Hebrews 4:12).

By identifying Himself as the one who holds the sharp two-edged sword, Jesus emphasizes His role as the ultimate judge and His authority to execute divine judgment.

The Commendation

Jesus continues His message with words of commendation for the church in Pergamum. Revelation 2:13 states:

> "I know your works, and where you dwell, where Satan's throne is. And you hold fast to My name, and did not deny My faith even in the days in which Antipas was My faithful martyr, who was killed among you, where Satan dwells."

- Works (ἔργον - Strong's G2041): Refers to the deeds and actions of the believers.

- Dwell (κατοικέω - Strong's G2730): Indicates their permanent residence in a place of great spiritual opposition.

- Satan's Throne (θρόνος - Strong's G2362): Likely refers to the center of pagan worship and idolatry in Pergamum, which included the great altar of Zeus.

- Hold Fast (κρατέω - Strong's G2902): Emphasizes their firm grip on their faith and commitment to Christ.

- Faithful Martyr (μάρτυς πιστός - Strong's G3144, G4103): Refers to Antipas, who remained faithful unto death.

Jesus acknowledges the difficult environment in which the Pergamum believers live, describing it as "where Satan's throne is." Despite this, they hold fast to His name and do not deny their faith, even in the face of severe persecution, exemplified by the martyrdom of Antipas.

The Correction

Despite their commendable faithfulness, Jesus has a significant correction for the church in Pergamum. Revelation 2:14-15 states:

> "But I have a few things against you, because you have there those who hold the doctrine of Balaam, who taught Balak to put a stumbling block before the children of Israel, to eat things sacrificed to idols, and to commit sexual immorality. Thus you also have those who hold the doctrine of the Nicolaitans, which thing I hate."

- Doctrine of Balaam (διδαχη□ Βαλαάμ - Strong's G1322, G903): Refers to the teachings that led Israel into idolatry and immorality (Numbers 22-25; 31:16).

- Stumbling Block (σκα□νδαλον - Strong's G4625): An obstacle leading to sin.

- Sexual Immorality (πορνει□α - Strong's G4202): Refers to illicit sexual behavior.

- Doctrine of the Nicolaitans (διδαχη□ Νικολαΐτης - Strong's G1322, G3531): Likely a sect promoting moral and doctrinal compromise.

Jesus rebukes the Pergamum church for tolerating the teachings of Balaam and the Nicolaitans, which promote idolatry and immorality. This correction highlights the danger of compromising with false teachings and the need for doctrinal purity.

The Call to Repent

Jesus calls the church in Pergamum to repentance. Revelation 2:16 states:

> "Repent, or else I will come to you quickly and will fight against them with the sword of My mouth."

- Repent (μετανοε□ω - Strong's G3340): Involves a change of mind and heart, turning away from their current state and returning to faithfulness.

- Sword of My Mouth (ῥομφαία ἐκ τοῦ στόματος - Strong's G4501, G1537, G4750): Represents the Word of God and Christ's authority to judge and correct.

Jesus commands the believers to repent of their compromises and false teachings. Failure to do so will result in His intervention and judgment, emphasizing the seriousness of their situation.

The Promise to Overcomers

Revelation 2:17 concludes the message with a promise to the overcomers:

> "He who has an ear, let him hear what the Spirit says to the churches. To him who overcomes I will give some of the hidden manna to eat. And I will give him a white stone, and on the stone a new name written which no one knows except him who receives it."

- Hidden Manna (μνα☐ - Strong's G3131): Symbolizes spiritual nourishment and the sustaining presence of Christ (Exodus 16:33-34; John 6:48-51).

- White Stone (λευκο☐ς ψῆφος - Strong's G3022, G5586): Likely a symbol of acquittal, acceptance, or victory.

- New Name (καινο☐ν ο☐νομα - Strong's G2537, G3686): Represents a new identity and relationship with Christ.

The promise to overcomers includes hidden manna, symbolizing spiritual sustenance, and a white stone with a new name, indicating acceptance, victory, and a personal relationship with Christ. These promises offer hope and encouragement to remain faithful.

Expository Insights

Examining the text through exhaustive Strong's Concordance reveals deeper meanings and connections:

- α☐γγελος (Strong's G32): While often translated as "angel," it can also mean "messenger," implying the leaders of the churches.

- ῥομφαία δίστομος ὀξεῖα (Strong's G4501, G1366, G3691): The sharp two-edged sword symbolizes the discerning and judging power of the Word of God.

- ἐ☐ργον (Strong's G2041): Emphasizes the tangible actions and ministries carried out by the church.

- κατοικε□ω (Strong's G2730): Indicates permanent residence in a challenging spiritual environment.

- θρο□νος (Strong's G2362): Refers to a seat of authority, here symbolizing the stronghold of Satanic influence.

- κρατε□ω (Strong's G2902): Emphasizes a firm grip on faith and commitment to Christ.

- μα□ρτυς πιστο□ς (Strong's G3144, G4103): Refers to a faithful witness, highlighting steadfast faithfulness unto death.

- διδαχη□ Βαλαάμ (Strong's G1322, G903): Indicates teachings that lead to idolatry and immorality.

- σκα□νδαλον (Strong's G4625): An obstacle or cause for sin.

- πορνει□α (Strong's G4202): Refers to sexual immorality.

- διδαχη□ Νικολαΐτης (Strong's G1322, G3531): Likely a sect promoting moral and doctrinal compromise.

- μετανοε□ω (Strong's G3340): True repentance involves a transformative change in direction and behavior.

- ῥομφαία ἐκ τοῦ στόματος (Strong's G4501, G1537, G4750): The sword from Jesus' mouth represents His authoritative Word.

- μνα□ (Strong's G3131): Hidden manna symbolizes spiritual nourishment and Christ's sustaining presence.

- λευκο□ς ψῆφος (Strong's G3022, G5586): A white stone represents acquittal, acceptance, or victory.

- καινο□ν ο□νομα (Strong's G2537, G3686): A new name symbolizes a new identity and relationship with Christ.

Practical Application

The message to the church in Pergamum holds timeless relevance for believers today. Key lessons include:

1. Holding Fast to Faith: Believers are called to remain steadfast in their faith, even in environments of intense spiritual opposition and pressure.

2. Rejecting Compromise: Compromising with false teachings and immoral practices is dangerous. Believers must uphold doctrinal purity and moral integrity.

3. Repentance and Correction: When compromise occurs, genuine repentance and correction are necessary to restore faithfulness.

4. Promise of Spiritual Nourishment and Victory: Jesus promises spiritual sustenance and ultimate victory

to those who overcome, offering hope and encouragement.

Conclusion

The message to the church in Pergamum in Revelation 2:12-17 provides a profound lesson on holding fast to faith despite external pressures. Through commendation, correction, and promise, Jesus calls believers to remain steadfast and reject compromise, holding onto the hope of spiritual nourishment and eternal victory. By examining these verses through an expository study with exhaustive Strong's Concordance, we uncover the depth of Jesus' message and its enduring relevance for the church today. As we heed His call to faithfulness and purity, we will experience the fullness of His presence and the eternal rewards He promises to those who overcome.

Lessons from the Seven Churches - Thyatira

In Revelation 2:18-29, Jesus addresses the church in Thyatira, the fourth of the seven churches in Asia Minor. This message emphasizes the importance of rejecting false teachings and immorality. By examining these verses through an expository study with exhaustive Strong's Concordance, we can uncover the deeper meanings and timeless lessons Jesus imparts to the believers in Thyatira and to Christians today.

The Greeting

Jesus begins His message to the church in Thyatira with a greeting that underscores His divine authority and omniscience. Revelation 2:18 states:

> "And to the angel of the church in Thyatira write, 'These things says the Son of God, who has eyes like a flame of fire, and His feet like fine brass.'"

- Angel (α□γγελος - Strong's G32): Refers to the messenger or leader of the church.

- Son of God (υἱο□ς τοῦ Θεοῦ - Strong's G5207, G2316): Emphasizes Jesus' divine nature and authority.

- Eyes like a flame of fire (ὀφθαλμοι□ αὐτοῦ ὡς φλόξ πυρός - Strong's G3788, G5613, G5395, G4442): Symbolizes Jesus' penetrating vision and ability to see all things.

- Feet like fine brass (πο□δες αὐτοῦ ο□μοιοι χαλκολιβάνω - Strong's G4228, G3664, G5474): Represents Jesus' strength, stability, and purity.

By identifying Himself as the Son of God with eyes like a flame of fire and feet like fine brass, Jesus emphasizes His divine authority, penetrating vision, and judgment.

The Commendation

Jesus continues His message with words of commendation for the church in Thyatira. Revelation 2:19 states:

> "I know your works, love, service, faith, and your patience; and as for your works, the last are more than the first."

- Works (ἔργον - Strong's G2041): Refers to the deeds and actions of the believers.

- Love (ἀγάπη - Strong's G26): Indicates their selfless, sacrificial love.

- Service (διακονία - Strong's G1248): Emphasizes their ministry and acts of service to others.

- Faith (πίστις - Strong's G4102): Denotes their trust and faithfulness to God.

- Patience (ὑπομονή - Strong's G5281): Highlights their endurance and perseverance.

Jesus acknowledges the commendable qualities of the Thyatiran believers, including their works, love, service, faith, and patience. Notably, He mentions that their latter works exceed their former ones, indicating growth and progress in their faith and ministry.

The Correction

Despite their commendable qualities, Jesus has a significant correction for the church in Thyatira. Revelation 2:20-23 states:

> "Nevertheless I have a few things against you, because you allow that woman Jezebel, who calls herself a

prophetess, to teach and seduce My servants to commit sexual immorality and eat things sacrificed to idols. And I gave her time to repent of her sexual immorality, and she did not repent. Indeed, I will cast her into a sickbed, and those who commit adultery with her into great tribulation, unless they repent of their deeds. I will kill her children with death, and all the churches shall know that I am He who searches the minds and hearts. And I will give to each one of you according to your works."

- Jezebel (Ιεζα βελ - Strong's G2403): Refers to a false prophetess leading the church into idolatry and immorality, reminiscent of the Old Testament Jezebel (1 Kings 16:31; 2 Kings 9:22).

- Sexual Immorality (πορνει α - Strong's G4202): Refers to illicit sexual behavior.

- Eat things sacrificed to idols (εἰδωλόθυτον - Strong's G1494): Indicates participation in idolatrous practices.

- Repent (μετανοε ω - Strong's G3340): Involves a change of mind and heart, turning away from sin.

- Sickbed (κλι νη - Strong's G2825): Symbolizes affliction and judgment.

- Adultery (μοιχει α - Strong's G3430): Used metaphorically for spiritual unfaithfulness.

- Minds (νεφρο□ς - Strong's G3510) and Hearts (καρδι□α - Strong's G2588): Indicate the inner thoughts and intentions.

Jesus rebukes the Thyatiran church for tolerating Jezebel, a false prophetess who leads believers into sexual immorality and idolatry. Despite being given time to repent, she has refused. Jesus warns of severe judgment for Jezebel and those who follow her teachings, emphasizing His ability to search minds and hearts and to judge according to deeds.

The Call to Hold Fast

Jesus calls the faithful believers in Thyatira to hold fast to their faith. Revelation 2:24-25 states:

> "Now to you I say, and to the rest in Thyatira, as many as do not have this doctrine, who have not known the depths of Satan, as they say, I will put on you no other burden. But hold fast what you have till I come."

- Depths of Satan (βαθυ□ς Σατανᾶ - Strong's G899, G4567): Refers to the deep and deceptive teachings of Jezebel, equated with satanic influence.

- Hold Fast (κρατε□ω - Strong's G2902): Emphasizes the need to firmly grasp and maintain their faith and commitment to Christ.

Jesus distinguishes the faithful believers who have not embraced Jezebel's false teachings and encourages them to hold fast to their faith until His return. He assures them that He will not impose additional burdens on them.

The Promise to Overcomers

Revelation 2:26-29 concludes the message with a promise to the overcomers:

> "And he who overcomes, and keeps My works until the end, to him I will give power over the nations— 'He shall rule them with a rod of iron; They shall be dashed to pieces like the potter's vessels'—as I also have received from My Father; and I will give him the morning star. He who has an ear, let him hear what the Spirit says to the churches."

- Overcomes (νικα□ω - Strong's G3528): Refers to those who remain faithful and victorious in their faith.

- Keeps My Works (τηρε□ω τα□ ε□ργα μου - Strong's G5083, G2041): Emphasizes maintaining obedience to Christ's commands and actions.

- Power over the Nations (ἐξουσία ἐπι□ τῶν ἐθνῶν - Strong's G1849, G1909, G1484): Indicates authority to rule with Christ in His kingdom.

- Rod of Iron (ῥάβδος σιδῆρα - Strong's G4464, G4603): Symbolizes firm and unyielding authority.

- Morning Star (πρωϊνο□ς ἀστὴρ - Strong's G3720, G792): Represents Jesus Himself, the bringer of hope and light (Revelation 22:16).

The promise to overcomers includes authority to rule with Christ and the gift of the morning star, symbolizing intimate fellowship with Jesus. These promises offer hope and encouragement to remain faithful and obedient.

Expository Insights

Examining the text through exhaustive Strong's Concordance reveals deeper meanings and connections:

- α□γγελος (Strong's G32): While often translated as "angel," it can also mean "messenger," implying the leaders of the churches.

- υίο□ς του̃ Θεου̃ (Strong's G5207, G2316): Emphasizes Jesus' divine nature and authority.

- ο'φθαλμοι□ αὐτου̃ ὡς φλόξ πυρός (Strong's G3788, G5613, G5395, G4442): The eyes like a flame of fire symbolize Jesus' penetrating vision and ability to see all things.

- πο□δες αὐτου̃ ο□μοιοι χαλκολιβάνω (Strong's G4228, G3664, G5474): The feet like fine brass represent Jesus' strength, stability, and purity.

- ε□ργον (Strong's G2041): Emphasizes the tangible actions and ministries carried out by the church.

- α'γάπη (Strong's G26): Indicates selfless, sacrificial love.

- διακονι□α (Strong's G1248): Emphasizes acts of service and ministry.

- πίστις (Strong's G4102): Denotes trust and faithfulness to God.

- ὑπομονή (Strong's G5281): Highlights endurance and perseverance.

- Ιεζαβελ (Strong's G2403): Refers to a false prophetess leading the church into idolatry and immorality.

- πορνεια (Strong's G4202): Refers to illicit sexual behavior.

- εἰδωλόθυτον (Strong's G1494): Indicates participation in idolatrous practices.

- μετανοεω (Strong's G3340): True repentance involves a transformative change in direction and behavior.

- κλινη (Strong's G2825): The sickbed symbolizes affliction and judgment.

- μοιχεια (Strong's G3430): Used metaphorically for spiritual unfaithfulness.

- νεφρος (Strong's G3510) and καρδια (Strong's G2588): Indicate the inner thoughts and intentions.

- βαθυς Σατανᾶ (Strong's G899, G4567): Refers to the deep and deceptive teachings of Jezebel, equated with satanic influence.

- κρατεω (Strong's G2902): Emphasizes a firm grip on faith and commitment to Christ.

- νικα ω (Strong's G3528): Refers to overcoming and remaining victorious in faith.

- τηρε ω τα ε ργα μου (Strong's G5083, G2041): Emphasizes maintaining obedience to Christ's commands and actions.

- ἐξουσία ἐπι τῶν ἐθνῶν (Strong's G1849, G1909, G1484): Indicates authority to rule with Christ in His kingdom.

- ῥάβδος σιδῆρα (Strong's G4464, G4603): Symbolizes firm and unyielding authority.

- πρωϊνο ς ἀστήρ (Strong's G3720, G792): Represents Jesus Himself, the bringer of hope and light.

Practical Application

The message to the church in Thyatira holds timeless relevance for believers today. Key lessons include:

1. Rejecting False Teachings and Immorality: Believers must remain vigilant against false teachings and immoral practices. Tolerance of such things can lead to spiritual downfall.

2. Repentance and Correction: Genuine repentance and correction are necessary when false teachings and immorality are present. Jesus calls His followers to turn away from sin and return to faithfulness.

3. Holding Fast to Faith: Believers are encouraged to hold fast to their faith and commitment to Christ, even in the face of challenges and opposition.

4. Promise of Authority and Fellowship: Jesus promises authority to rule with Him and the gift of the morning star to those who overcome, offering hope and encouragement for remaining faithful.

Conclusion

The message to the church in Thyatira in Revelation 2:18-29 provides a profound lesson on rejecting false teachings and immorality. Through commendation, correction, and promise, Jesus calls believers to maintain doctrinal purity and moral integrity, holding fast to their faith and commitment to Him. By examining these verses through an expository study with exhaustive Strong's Concordance, we uncover the depth of Jesus' message and its enduring relevance for the church today. As we heed His call to faithfulness and purity, we will experience the fullness of His presence and the eternal rewards He promises to those who overcome.

Lessons from the Seven Churches - Sardis

In Revelation 3:1-6, Jesus addresses the church in Sardis, the fifth of the seven churches in Asia Minor. This message emphasizes the importance of spiritual vigilance and repentance. By examining these verses through an expository study with exhaustive Strong's Concordance, we can uncover the deeper meanings and timeless lessons Jesus imparts to the believers in Sardis and to Christians today.

The Greeting

Jesus begins His message to the church in Sardis with a greeting that underscores His authority and omniscience. Revelation 3:1 states:

> "And to the angel of the church in Sardis write, 'These things says He who has the seven Spirits of God and the seven stars: "I know your works, that you have a name that you are alive, but you are dead."'"

- Angel (αγγελος - Strong's G32): Refers to the messenger or leader of the church.

- Seven Spirits of God (τα επτα πνεύματα τοῦ Θεοῦ - Strong's G2033, G4151, G2316): Represents the fullness and completeness of the Holy Spirit (Isaiah 11:2).

- Seven Stars (τα επτα ἀστέρες - Strong's G2033, G792): Symbolizes the leaders of the seven churches (Revelation 1:20).

By identifying Himself as the one who has the seven Spirits of God and the seven stars, Jesus emphasizes His divine authority, the completeness of the Holy Spirit, and His sovereign oversight of the churches.

The Commendation and Rebuke

Jesus continues His message with a combined commendation and rebuke for the church in Sardis. Revelation 3:1b-2 states:

> "I know your works, that you have a name that you are alive, but you are dead. Be watchful, and strengthen the things which remain, that are ready to die, for I have not found your works perfect before God."

- Works (ε□ργον - Strong's G2041): Refers to the deeds and actions of the believers.

- Name (o□νομα - Strong's G3686): Indicates reputation or identity.

- Alive (ζα□ω - Strong's G2198) but Dead (νεκρο□ς - Strong's G3498): Contrasts their outward appearance of life with their true spiritual state of death.

- Watchful (γρηγορε□ω - Strong's G1127): Calls for vigilance and alertness.

- Strengthen (στηρι□ζω - Strong's G4741): Emphasizes the need to support and revive what remains.

Jesus acknowledges the church's reputation for being alive, but He reveals their true spiritual condition as being dead. He calls them to be watchful and to strengthen what remains, indicating that there is still hope for revival if they heed His warning.

The Call to Remember, Hold Fast, and Repent

Jesus provides a threefold remedy for the Sardian church's condition: remember, hold fast, and repent. Revelation 3:3 states:

> "Remember therefore how you have received and heard; hold fast and repent. Therefore if you will not watch, I will come upon you as a thief, and you will not know what hour I will come upon you."

- Remember (μνημονευ□ω - Strong's G3421): Calls the believers to recall their initial reception of the gospel and their early faith.

- Hold Fast (τηρε□ω - Strong's G5083): Emphasizes the need to keep and maintain their faith and commitment.

- Repent (μετανοε□ω - Strong's G3340): Involves a change of mind and heart, turning away from their current state and returning to faithfulness.

- Watch (γρηγορε□ω - Strong's G1127): Reiterates the call for vigilance and readiness.

Jesus urges the Sardian believers to remember their initial faith, hold fast to it, and repent of their current state. He warns that if they do not remain watchful, He will come upon them unexpectedly, like a thief, indicating sudden judgment.

The Promise to the Faithful Remnant

Revelation 3:4-5 provides a promise to the faithful remnant in Sardis:

> "You have a few names even in Sardis who have not defiled their garments; and they shall walk with Me in white, for they are worthy. He who overcomes shall be clothed in white garments, and I will not blot out his name from the Book of Life; but I will confess his name before My Father and before His angels."

- Names (ὄνομα - Strong's G3686): Refers to individuals who have remained faithful.

- Defiled (μολύνω - Strong's G3435): Indicates being stained or polluted, particularly by sin.

- Garments (ἱμάτιον - Strong's G2440): Symbolizes one's moral and spiritual state.

- White (λευκός - Strong's G3022): Represents purity, righteousness, and victory.

- Overcomes (νικάω - Strong's G3528): Refers to those who remain faithful and victorious in their faith.

- Book of Life (βίβλος τῆς ζωῆς - Strong's G976, G2222): Represents the register of those who have eternal life.

- Confess (ἐξομολογέω - Strong's G1843): Indicates acknowledgment or proclamation.

Jesus acknowledges that there are a few individuals in Sardis who have not defiled their garments, meaning they have remained faithful and pure. He promises that these overcomers will be clothed in white garments, symbolizing their righteousness and victory. Additionally, He assures them that their names will not be blotted out from the Book of Life and that He will confess their names before His Father and the angels, signifying their acceptance and acknowledgment in the heavenly realm.

The Concluding Admonition

Revelation 3:6 concludes the message with a general admonition:

> "He who has an ear, let him hear what the Spirit says to the churches."

- Ear (οὖς - Strong's G3775): Symbolizes the capacity to hear and understand.

- Hear (ἀκούω - Strong's G191): Calls for attentive listening and obedience to the message.

This concluding admonition emphasizes the importance of heeding the message, not just for the church in Sardis, but for all believers. It calls for spiritual receptivity and responsiveness to the Holy Spirit's guidance.

Expository Insights

Examining the text through exhaustive Strong's Concordance reveals deeper meanings and connections:

- α□γγελος (Strong's G32): While often translated as "angel," it can also mean "messenger," implying the leaders of the churches.

- τα□ ἑπτα□ πνεύματα τοῦ Θεοῦ (Strong's G2033, G4151, G2316): Represents the fullness and completeness of the Holy Spirit.

- τα□ ἑπτα□ ἀστέρες (Strong's G2033, G792): Symbolizes the leaders of the seven churches.

- ε□ργον (Strong's G2041): Emphasizes the tangible actions and ministries carried out by the church.

- ο□νομα (Strong's G3686): Indicates reputation or identity.

- ζα□ω (Strong's G2198) and νεκρο□ς (Strong's G3498): Contrasts their outward appearance of life with their true spiritual state of death.

- γρηγορε□ω (Strong's G1127): Calls for vigilance and alertness.

- στηρι□ζω (Strong's G4741): Emphasizes the need to support and revive what remains.

- μνημονευ□ω (Strong's G3421): Calls the believers to recall their initial reception of the gospel and their early faith.

- τηρε□ω (Strong's G5083): Emphasizes the need to keep and maintain their faith and commitment.

- μετανοε□ω (Strong's G3340): True repentance involves a transformative change in direction and behavior.

- μολυ□νω (Strong's G3435): Indicates being stained or polluted, particularly by sin.

- ἱμάτιον (Strong's G2440): Symbolizes one's moral and spiritual state.

- λευκο□ς (Strong's G3022): Represents purity, righteousness, and victory.

- νικα□ω (Strong's G3528): Refers to overcoming and remaining victorious in faith.

- βι□βλος τῆς ζωῆς (Strong's G976, G2222): Represents the register of those who have eternal life.

- εξομολογέω (Strong's G1843): Indicates acknowledgment or proclamation.

- οὖς (Strong's G3775) and ἀκούω (Strong's G191): Symbolizes the capacity to hear and understand and calls for attentive listening and obedience.

Practical Application

The message to the church in Sardis holds timeless relevance for believers today. Key lessons include:

1. Spiritual Vigilance: Believers must remain spiritually vigilant and alert, continually examining their faith and actions to ensure they are truly alive in Christ.

2. Repentance and Renewal: When spiritual complacency and deadness are present, genuine repentance and renewal are necessary. Jesus calls His followers to remember their initial faith, hold fast to it, and repent of their current state.

3. Faithful Remnant: Even in spiritually dead environments, there can be a faithful remnant who remain pure and committed to Christ. These individuals are promised eternal rewards and acknowledgment in the heavenly realm.

4. Heeding the Spirit's Message: Believers are called to listen attentively to the Holy Spirit's guidance and to respond with obedience and faithfulness.

Conclusion

The message to the church in Sardis in Revelation 3:1-6 provides a profound lesson on spiritual vigilance and repentance. Through commendation, correction, and promise, Jesus calls believers to remain alert, to strengthen what remains, and to repent of any spiritual deadness. By examining these verses through an expository study with exhaustive Strong's Concordance, we uncover the depth of Jesus' message and its enduring relevance for the church today. As we heed His call to vigilance and repentance, we will experience the fullness of His presence and the eternal rewards He promises to those who overcome.

Lessons from the Seven Churches - Philadelphia

In Revelation 3:7-13, Jesus addresses the church in Philadelphia, the sixth of the seven churches in Asia Minor. This message emphasizes the importance of perseverance and faithfulness. By examining these verses through an expository study with exhaustive Strong's Concordance, we can uncover the deeper meanings and timeless lessons Jesus imparts to the believers in Philadelphia and to Christians today.

The Greeting

Jesus begins His message to the church in Philadelphia with a greeting that underscores His authority and holiness. Revelation 3:7 states:

> "And to the angel of the church in Philadelphia write, 'These things says He who is holy, He who is true, He who has the key of David, He who opens and no one shuts, and shuts and no one opens.'"

- Angel (ἄγγελος - Strong's G32): Refers to the messenger or leader of the church.

- Holy (ἅγιος - Strong's G40): Emphasizes Jesus' purity and separation from sin.

- True (ἀληθινός - Strong's G228): Highlights Jesus' authenticity and reliability.

- Key of David (κλεὶς Δαυίδ - Strong's G2807, G1138): Symbolizes authority over the kingdom of David, indicating Christ's messianic authority (Isaiah 22:22).

- Opens and no one shuts, and shuts and no one opens (ἀνοίγω καὶ οὐδεὶς κλείει, καὶ κλείω καὶ οὐδεὶς ἀνοίγει - Strong's G455, G3762, G2808, G3762, G455): Represents Jesus' sovereign control and authority.

By identifying Himself as holy and true, and as the one who holds the key of David, Jesus emphasizes His divine authority and His control over the opportunities and destinies of the believers.

The Commendation

Jesus continues His message with words of commendation for the church in Philadelphia. Revelation 3:8 states:

> "I know your works. See, I have set before you an open door, and no one can shut it; for you have a little strength, have kept My word, and have not denied My name."

- Works (ἔργον - Strong's G2041): Refers to the deeds and actions of the believers.

- Open Door (ἀνοίγω θύρα - Strong's G455, G2374): Symbolizes opportunities for ministry and service.

- Little Strength (μικρο□ ς δύναμις - Strong's G3398, G1411): Indicates their limited power or resources.

- Kept (τηρε□ ω - Strong's G5083): Emphasizes their obedience to Jesus' word.

- Not Denied (οὐκ ἀρνέομαι - Strong's G3756, G720): Highlights their steadfastness in maintaining their faith and allegiance to Jesus.

Jesus acknowledges the works of the Philadelphia believers and commends them for their perseverance and faithfulness, despite having limited strength. He emphasizes the open door of opportunity He has set before them, which no one can shut, signifying their faithful ministry and witness.

The Promise of Protection

Jesus promises protection and vindication for the faithful believers in Philadelphia. Revelation 3:9-10 states:

> "Indeed I will make those of the synagogue of Satan, who say they are Jews and are not, but lie—indeed I will make them come and worship before your feet, and to know that I have loved you. Because you have kept My command to persevere, I also will keep you from the hour of trial which shall come upon the whole world, to test those who dwell on the earth."

- Synagogue of Satan (Συναγωγη□ τοῦ Σατανᾶ - Strong's G4864, G4567): Refers to those who falsely claim to be Jews but are not truly following God.

- Worship before your feet (προσκυνε□ ω ἐνώπιον τοῦ πόδες - Strong's G4352, G1799, G4228): Indicates acknowledgment of their faithful witness and God's love for them.

- Loved (ἠγάπησα - Strong's G25): Emphasizes Jesus' love and approval of the believers.

- Kept My Command to Persevere (τηρε□ ω λόγος ὑπομονή - Strong's G5083, G3056, G5281): Refers to their obedience to Jesus' command to endure.

- Keep you from the hour of trial (τηρε□ ω ἐκ η□ ρα πειρασμός - Strong's G5083, G1537, G5610, G3986): Promises protection from the time of testing and tribulation.

Jesus assures the Philadelphia believers that their faithfulness will be vindicated, and their enemies will recognize God's love for them. He promises to protect them from the coming hour of trial that will test those who dwell on the earth, highlighting His care and provision for His faithful followers.

The Call to Hold Fast

Jesus calls the faithful believers in Philadelphia to hold fast to their faith. Revelation 3:11 states:

> "Behold, I am coming quickly! Hold fast what you have, that no one may take your crown."

- Coming Quickly (ἔρχομαι ταχύ - Strong's G2064, G5035): Indicates the imminence of Jesus' return.

- Hold Fast (κρατέω - Strong's G2902): Emphasizes the need to firmly grasp and maintain their faith and commitment.

- Crown (στέφανος - Strong's G4735): Represents the reward of victory and faithfulness.

Jesus urges the Philadelphia believers to hold fast to what they have, so that no one may take their crown. This call to perseverance underscores the importance of maintaining their faith and commitment until His return.

The Promise to Overcomers

Revelation 3:12-13 concludes the message with a promise to the overcomers:

> "He who overcomes, I will make him a pillar in the temple of My God, and he shall go out no more. I will write on him the name of My God and the name of the city of My God, the New Jerusalem, which comes down out of heaven from My God. And I will write on him My new name. He who has an ear, let him hear what the Spirit says to the churches."

- Overcomes (νικάω - Strong's G3528): Refers to those who remain faithful and victorious in their faith.

- Pillar (στύλος - Strong's G4769): Symbolizes stability, permanence, and honor in God's presence.

- Temple (ναός - Strong's G3485): Refers to the dwelling place of God.

- Go out no more (ἔρχομαι ἔξω οὐκ ἔτι - Strong's G2064, G1854, G3765): Indicates eternal security and permanence.

- Name of My God (ὄνομα τοῦ Θεοῦ μου - Strong's G3686, G2316): Represents belonging to God and being identified with Him.

- New Jerusalem (καινὸς Ἰερουσαλήμ - Strong's G2537, G2419): Refers to the eternal city of God, the ultimate destination of the faithful.

- My new name (καινὸς ὄνομα μου - Strong's G2537, G3686): Indicates a new identity and relationship with Christ.

The promise to overcomers includes being made a pillar in the temple of God, symbolizing stability, honor, and eternal security. They will have the name of God, the name of the New Jerusalem, and Jesus' new name written on them, signifying their belonging to God and their eternal relationship with Him.

Expository Insights

Examining the text through exhaustive Strong's Concordance reveals deeper meanings and connections:

- α□γγελος (Strong's G32): While often translated as "angel," it can also mean "messenger," implying the leaders of the churches.

- α□γιος (Strong's G40): Emphasizes Jesus' purity and separation from sin.

- αληθινός (Strong's G228): Highlights Jesus' authenticity and reliability.

- κλει□ς Δαυιδ (Strong's G2807, G1138): Symbolizes authority over the kingdom of David, indicating Christ's messianic authority.

- ανοίγω θύρα (Strong's G455, G2374): Symbolizes opportunities for ministry and service.

- μικρο□ς δύναμις (Strong's G3398, G1411): Indicates their limited power or resources.

- τηρε□ω (Strong's G5083): Emphasizes the need to keep and maintain their faith and commitment.

- ουκ αρνέομαι (Strong's G3756, G720): Highlights their steadfastness in maintaining their faith and allegiance to Jesus.

- Συνα

γωγη☐ τοῦ Σατανᾶ (Strong's G4864, G4567): Refers to those who falsely claim to be Jews but are not truly following God.

- προσκυνε☐ ω ἐνώπιον τοῦ πόδες (Strong's G4352, G1799, G4228): Indicates acknowledgment of their faithful witness and God's love for them.

- ἠγάπησα (Strong's G25): Emphasizes Jesus' love and approval of the believers.

- τηρε☐ ω λόγος ὑπομονή (Strong's G5083, G3056, G5281): Refers to their obedience to Jesus' command to endure.

- τηρε☐ ω ἐκ η☐ ρα πειρασμός (Strong's G5083, G1537, G5610, G3986): Promises protection from the time of testing and tribulation.

- ε☐ ρχομαι ταχύ (Strong's G2064, G5035): Indicates the imminence of Jesus' return.

- κρατε☐ ω (Strong's G2902): Emphasizes a firm grip on faith and commitment.

- στέφανος (Strong's G4735): Represents the reward of victory and faithfulness.

- νικα☐ ω (Strong's G3528): Refers to overcoming and remaining victorious in faith.

- στυ☐ λος (Strong's G4769): Symbolizes stability, permanence, and honor in God's presence.

- ναο□ ς (Strong's G3485): Refers to the dwelling place of God.

- ε□ ρχομαι ε□ ξω ου□κ ε□ τι (Strong's G2064, G1854, G3765): Indicates eternal security and permanence.

- ο□ νομα του̃ Θεου̃ μου (Strong's G3686, G2316): Represents belonging to God and being identified with Him.

- καινο□ ς Ιερουσαλη□ μ (Strong's G2537, G2419): Refers to the eternal city of God, the ultimate destination of the faithful.

- καινο□ ς ο□ νομα μου (Strong's G2537, G3686): Indicates a new identity and relationship with Christ.

Practical Application

The message to the church in Philadelphia holds timeless relevance for believers today. Key lessons include:

1. Perseverance and Faithfulness: Believers are called to persevere and remain faithful, even with limited strength. Jesus commends those who keep His word and do not deny His name.

2. Opportunities for Ministry: Jesus opens doors of opportunity for ministry and service that no one can shut. Believers should be vigilant and take advantage of these opportunities.

3. Protection and Vindication: Jesus promises protection from trials and vindication before their enemies. Believers can trust in His care and provision.

4. Eternal Rewards: Jesus promises eternal rewards and a secure place in His presence for those who overcome. This includes being made a pillar in the temple of God and having His name written on them.

Conclusion

The message to the church in Philadelphia in Revelation 3:7-13 provides a profound lesson on perseverance and faithfulness. Through commendation, promise, and a call to hold fast, Jesus encourages believers to remain steadfast and faithful, taking advantage of the opportunities He provides. By examining these verses through an expository study with exhaustive Strong's Concordance, we uncover the depth of Jesus' message and its enduring relevance for the church today. As we heed His call to perseverance and faithfulness, we will experience the fullness of His presence and the eternal rewards He promises to those who overcome.

Lessons from the Seven Churches - Laodicea

In Revelation 3:14-22, Jesus addresses the church in Laodicea, the seventh and final church in Asia Minor. This message is a stark warning about the dangers of lukewarm faith. By examining these verses through an expository study with exhaustive Strong's Concordance, we can uncover the deeper meanings and timeless lessons Jesus imparts to the believers in Laodicea and to Christians today.

The Greeting

Jesus begins His message to the church in Laodicea with a greeting that underscores His authority and faithfulness. Revelation 3:14 states:

> "And to the angel of the church of the Laodiceans write, 'These things says the Amen, the Faithful and True Witness, the Beginning of the creation of God.'"

- Angel (α□γγελος - Strong's G32): Refers to the messenger or leader of the church.

- Amen (Αμη□ν - Strong's G281): Signifies truth and certainty, emphasizing Jesus' trustworthiness.

- Faithful and True Witness (ὁ μάρτυς ὁ πιστὸς καὶ□ αληθινός - Strong's G3144, G4103, G228): Highlights Jesus' reliability and His role in testifying to the truth.

- Beginning of the creation of God (ἡ αρχη□ τῆς κτίσεως τοῦ Θεοῦ - Strong's G746, G2937, G2316): Indicates Jesus' preeminence and authority over all creation.

By identifying Himself as the Amen, the Faithful and True Witness, and the Beginning of the creation of God, Jesus emphasizes His divine authority, reliability, and preeminence.

The Rebuke

Jesus' message to the church in Laodicea contains a strong rebuke. Revelation 3:15-17 states:

> "I know your works, that you are neither cold nor hot. I could wish you were cold or hot. So then, because you are lukewarm, and neither cold nor hot, I will vomit you out of My mouth. Because you say, 'I am rich, have become wealthy, and have need of nothing'—and do not know that you are wretched, miserable, poor, blind, and naked."

- Works (ε□ργον - Strong's G2041): Refers to the deeds and actions of the believers.

- Cold (ψυχρο□ς - Strong's G5593): Symbolizes spiritual coldness or indifference.

- Hot (ζεστο□ς - Strong's G2200): Symbolizes spiritual fervor and zeal.

- Lukewarm (χλιαρο□ς - Strong's G5513): Indicates a state of spiritual complacency and indifference.

- Vomit (ἐμέω - Strong's G1692): Represents Jesus' rejection of their lukewarm state.

- Rich (πλου□σιος - Strong's G4145), Wealthy (πλουτε□ω - Strong's G4147), Need of Nothing (χρει□α - Strong's G5532): Reflects their self-sufficiency and complacency.

- Wretched (ταλαιπωρο□ ς - Strong's G5005), Miserable (ελεεινός - Strong's G1652), Poor (πτωχός - Strong's G4434), Blind (τυφλός - Strong's G5185), Naked (γυμνός - Strong's G1131): Describes their true spiritual condition.

Jesus rebukes the Laodicean church for being neither cold nor hot, but lukewarm, and thus repulsive to Him. Their self-perception of being rich and self-sufficient is contrasted with their true spiritual state of wretchedness, misery, poverty, blindness, and nakedness.

The Counsel

Jesus offers counsel to the Laodicean believers on how to remedy their spiritual condition. Revelation 3:18 states:

> "I counsel you to buy from Me gold refined in the fire, that you may be rich; and white garments, that you may be clothed, that the shame of your nakedness may not be revealed; and anoint your eyes with eye salve, that you may see."

- Buy (ἀγοράζω - Strong's G59): Indicates the need to acquire spiritual riches from Jesus.

- Gold Refined in the Fire (χρυσι□ ον πυρο□ ω - Strong's G5557, G4448): Symbolizes genuine faith and spiritual wealth.

- White Garments (λευκο□ς ἱμάτιον - Strong's G3022, G2440): Represents righteousness and purity.

- Shame of Your Nakedness (αἰσχύνη γυμνότης - Strong's G152, G1132): Refers to their exposed spiritual condition.

- Eye Salve (κολλου□ριον - Strong's G2854): Symbolizes spiritual insight and discernment.

Jesus counsels the Laodicean believers to seek true spiritual wealth, righteousness, and insight from Him. This involves a transformative process of refining, clothing, and healing.

The Call to Repent

Jesus calls the Laodicean church to repentance. Revelation 3:19 states:

> "As many as I love, I rebuke and chasten. Therefore be zealous and repent."

- Love (φιλε□ω - Strong's G5368): Emphasizes Jesus' affection and concern for His followers.

- Rebuke (ἐλέγχω - Strong's G1651) and Chasten (παιδεύω - Strong's G3811): Indicates corrective discipline intended to restore.

- Zealous (ζηλευ□ω - Strong's G2206): Calls for fervent commitment and passion.

- Repent (μετανοε□ω - Strong's G3340): Involves a change of mind and heart, turning away from sin and returning to God.

Jesus' rebuke and discipline are motivated by His love, and He calls the Laodicean believers to respond with zeal and repentance, reigniting their spiritual fervor and commitment.

The Promise to Overcomers

Revelation 3:20-22 concludes the message with a promise to the overcomers:

> "Behold, I stand at the door and knock. If anyone hears My voice and opens the door, I will come in to him and dine with him, and he with Me. To him who overcomes I will grant to sit with Me on My throne, as I also overcame and sat down with My Father on His throne. He who has an ear, let him hear what the Spirit says to the churches."

- Stand (ἱ□στημι - Strong's G2476) and Knock (κρούω - Strong's G2925): Indicates Jesus' invitation and desire for fellowship.

- Hears (ἀκούω - Strong's G191) and Opens (ἀνοίγω - Strong's G455): Calls for responsive action to Jesus' invitation.

- Dine (δειπνε□ω - Strong's G1172): Represents intimate fellowship and communion.

- Overcomes (νικα□ω - Strong's G3528): Refers to those who remain faithful and victorious in their faith.

- Sit with Me on My Throne (κα□ θημαι συ□ν ἐμοι□ ἐπι□ ὁ θρόνος - Strong's G2521, G4862, G1698, G1909, G3588, G2362): Indicates sharing in Jesus' authority and victory.

Jesus offers a gracious invitation to fellowship with Him, standing at the door and knocking. He promises intimate fellowship and the privilege of sharing in His authority and victory to those who overcome.

Expository Insights

Examining the text through exhaustive Strong's Concordance reveals deeper meanings and connections:

- α□γγελος (Strong's G32): While often translated as "angel," it can also mean "messenger," implying the leaders of the churches.

- Αμη□ν (Strong's G281): Signifies truth and certainty, emphasizing Jesus' trustworthiness.

- ὁ μάρτυς ὁ πιστός και□ ἀληθινός (Strong's G3144, G4103, G228): Highlights Jesus' reliability and His role in testifying to the truth.

- ἡ ἀρχη□ τῆς κτίσεως του̃ Θεου̃ (Strong's G746, G2937, G2316): Indicates Jesus' preeminence and authority over all creation.

- ἔ ργον (Strong's G2041): Emphasizes the tangible actions and ministries carried out by the church.

- ψυχρο□ς (Strong's G5593): Symbolizes spiritual coldness or indifference.

- ζεστο□ς (Strong's G2200): Symbolizes spiritual fervor and zeal.

- χλιαρο□ς (Strong's G5513): Indicates a state of spiritual complacency and indifference.

- ἐμέω (Strong's G1692

): Represents Jesus' rejection of their lukewarm state.

- πλου□σιος (Strong's G4145), πλουτε□ω (Strong's G4147), χρει□α (Strong's G5532): Reflects their self-sufficiency and complacency.

- ταλαιπωρο□ς (Strong's G5005), ἐλεεινός (Strong's G1652), πτωχός (Strong's G4434), τυφλός (Strong's G5185), γυμνός (Strong's G1131): Describes their true spiritual condition.

- ἀγοράζω (Strong's G59): Indicates the need to acquire spiritual riches from Jesus.

- χρυσι□ον πυρο□ω (Strong's G5557, G4448): Symbolizes genuine faith and spiritual wealth.

- λευκο□ς ἱμάτιον (Strong's G3022, G2440): Represents righteousness and purity.

- αἰσχύνη γυμνότης (Strong's G152, G1132): Refers to their exposed spiritual condition.

- κολλου□ριον (Strong's G2854): Symbolizes spiritual insight and discernment.

- φιλε□ω (Strong's G5368): Emphasizes Jesus' affection and concern for His followers.

- ἐλέγχω (Strong's G1651) and παιδεύω (Strong's G3811): Indicates corrective discipline intended to restore.

- ζηλευ□ω (Strong's G2206): Calls for fervent commitment and passion.

- μετανοε□ω (Strong's G3340): True repentance involves a transformative change in direction and behavior.

- ἱ□στημι (Strong's G2476) and κρούω (Strong's G2925): Indicates Jesus' invitation and desire for fellowship.

- ἀκούω (Strong's G191) and ἀνοίγω (Strong's G455): Calls for responsive action to Jesus' invitation.

- δειπνε□ω (Strong's G1172): Represents intimate fellowship and communion.

- νικα□ω (Strong's G3528): Refers to overcoming and remaining victorious in faith.

- κα□θημαι συ□ν ἐμοι□ ἐπι□ ὁ θρόνος (Strong's G2521, G4862, G1698, G1909, G3588, G2362): Indicates sharing in Jesus' authority and victory.

Practical Application

The message to the church in Laodicea holds timeless relevance for believers today. Key lessons include:

1. Avoiding Lukewarm Faith: Believers must guard against spiritual complacency and indifference. Lukewarm faith is repulsive to Jesus and leads to spiritual deadness.

2. Recognizing True Spiritual Condition: Self-sufficiency and complacency can blind believers to their true spiritual state. Jesus calls for an honest assessment and recognition of our need for Him.

3. Seeking Spiritual Riches: True spiritual wealth, righteousness, and insight come from Jesus. Believers must seek these from Him through a transformative process of refining, clothing, and healing.

4. Responding to Discipline with Repentance: Jesus' rebuke and discipline are motivated by His love. Believers should respond with zeal and repentance, reigniting their spiritual fervor and commitment.

5. Opening the Door to Fellowship: Jesus desires intimate fellowship with His followers. Believers must be responsive to His invitation, opening the door to a deeper relationship with Him.

6. Eternal Rewards for Overcomers: Jesus promises intimate fellowship, sharing in His authority, and eternal

rewards to those who overcome. Believers can look forward to these blessings as they remain faithful.

Conclusion

The message to the church in Laodicea in Revelation 3:14-22 provides a profound lesson on avoiding lukewarm faith. Through rebuke, counsel, and promise, Jesus calls believers to recognize their true spiritual condition, seek spiritual riches from Him, and respond to His discipline with repentance. By examining these verses through an expository study with exhaustive Strong's Concordance, we uncover the depth of Jesus' message and its enduring relevance for the church today. As we heed His call to avoid lukewarm faith and embrace a fervent, committed relationship with Him, we will experience the fullness of His presence and the eternal rewards He promises to those who overcome.

CHAPTER 04

THE THRONE ROOM VISION

Revelation 4 presents a majestic vision of God's throne room, highlighting the sovereignty and divine authority of Jesus Christ. This chapter provides a vivid depiction of heavenly worship, emphasizing the holiness and eternal reign of God. By examining these verses through an expository study with exhaustive Strong's Concordance, we can uncover the deeper meanings and profound truths revealed in this vision.

The Invitation to the Throne Room

Revelation 4:1 begins with an invitation for John to enter the heavenly realm and witness the vision:

> "After these things I looked, and behold, a door standing open in heaven. And the first voice which I heard was like a trumpet speaking with me, saying, 'Come up here, and I will show you things which must take place after this.'"

- Looked (βλε□πω - Strong's G991): Indicates John's attentive and expectant gaze.

- Door (θυ□ρα - Strong's G2374): Symbolizes access to the divine realm.

- Heaven (οὐρανός - Strong's G3772): Refers to the abode of God.

- Voice (φωνη□ - Strong's G5456): Represents divine communication.

- Trumpet (σα□λπιγξ - Strong's G4536): Symbolizes a clear and authoritative call.

- Come Up Here (ἀναβαίνω ὦδε - Strong's G305, G5602): An invitation to ascend to the heavenly realm.

- Show (δει□κνυμι - Strong's G1166): Indicates a divine revelation of future events.

John is invited to enter the open door in heaven and witness the revelation of things to come. This invitation underscores the divine initiative in revealing heavenly mysteries to humankind.

The Vision of the Throne

Revelation 4:2-3 describes the vision of God's throne:

> "Immediately I was in the Spirit; and behold, a throne set in heaven, and One sat on the throne. And He who sat there was like a jasper and a sardius stone in appearance; and there was a rainbow around the throne, in appearance like an emerald."

- In the Spirit (ἐν πνεύματι - Strong's G1722, G4151): Indicates a state of spiritual vision and revelation.

- Throne (θρο□νος - Strong's G2362): Represents God's sovereign authority and rule.

- Sat (καθη□μαι - Strong's G2521): Denotes a position of authority and judgment.

- Jasper (ια□σπιδ - Strong's G2393): A precious stone symbolizing purity and majesty.

- Sardius (σα□ρδιος - Strong's G4555): A reddish stone symbolizing God's fiery judgment and glory.

- Rainbow (□ρις - Strong's G2463): Represents God's covenant faithfulness and mercy.

- Emerald (σμαραγδι□ν - Strong's G4664): A green stone symbolizing life and renewal.

John sees a vision of God's throne, radiant with the appearance of jasper and sardius stones, and encircled by a rainbow resembling an emerald. This imagery emphasizes God's majesty, purity, and covenant faithfulness.

The Twenty-Four Elders

Revelation 4:4 describes the twenty-four elders around the throne:

> "Around the throne were twenty-four thrones, and on the thrones I saw twenty-four elders sitting, clothed in white robes; and they had crowns of gold on their heads."

- Thrones (θρο□νος - Strong's G2362): Represents positions of authority and judgment.

- Twenty-Four (εἴκοσι τέσσαρες - Strong's G1501, G5064): Symbolizes completeness and representation of God's people.

- Elders (πρεσβύτερος - Strong's G4245): Indicates mature, authoritative figures.

- Clothed (περιβάλλω - Strong's G4016): Refers to being arrayed or dressed.

- White Robes (λευκός ἱμάτιον - Strong's G3022, G2440): Represents purity and righteousness.

- Crowns of Gold (στέφανος χρυσοῦς - Strong's G4735, G5557): Symbolizes victory and honor.

The twenty-four elders represent the fullness of God's people, clothed in white robes symbolizing purity and righteousness, and wearing crowns of gold indicating their victorious status and honor.

The Four Living Creatures

Revelation 4:6-8 introduces the four living creatures:

> "Before the throne there was a sea of glass, like crystal. And in the midst of the throne, and around the throne, were four living creatures full of eyes in front and in back. The first living creature was like a lion, the second living creature like a calf, the third living creature had a face like a man, and the fourth living creature was like a flying eagle. The four living creatures, each having six wings, were full of eyes

around and within. And they do not rest day or night, saying: 'Holy, holy, holy, Lord God Almighty, Who was and is and is to come!'"

- Sea of Glass (θα□λασσα ὑάλινος - Strong's G2281, G5193): Symbolizes purity, clarity, and peace.

- Living Creatures (ζῶον - Strong's G2226): Represent angelic beings or cherubim.

- Eyes (ὀφθαλμός - Strong's G3788): Symbolize knowledge and vigilance.

- Lion (λε□ων - Strong's G3023), Calf (μόσχος - Strong's G3448), Man (α□νθρωπος - Strong's G444), Eagle (ἀετός - Strong's G105): Represent strength, service, intelligence, and swiftness, respectively.

- Six Wings (ἑ□ξ πτερύγιον - Strong's G1803, G4420): Indicate mobility and readiness to serve.

- Holy, Holy, Holy (α□γιος, α□γιος, α□γιος - Strong's G40): Emphasizes the absolute holiness of God.

- Lord God Almighty (Κυ□ριος Θεο□ς παντοκράτωρ - Strong's G2962, G2316, G3841): Declares God's supreme authority and power.

- Who Was and Is and Is to Come (ὁ ἦν και□ ὁ ω□ν και□ ὁ ἐρχόμενος - Strong's G1510, G3739, G2064): Affirms God's eternal existence.

The four living creatures, each with distinct appearances and covered with eyes, continuously worship God, declaring His holiness and eternal reign. Their ceaseless praise emphasizes God's supreme authority and the perpetual adoration He receives in heaven.

The Worship of the Elders

Revelation 4:9-11 describes the worship of the twenty-four elders:

> "Whenever the living creatures give glory and honor and thanks to Him who sits on the throne, who lives forever and ever, the twenty-four elders fall down before Him who sits on the throne and worship Him who lives forever and ever, and cast their crowns before the throne, saying: 'You are worthy, O Lord, to receive glory and honor and power; For You created all things, And by Your will they exist and were created.'"

- Glory (δο□ξα - Strong's G1391), Honor (τιμή - Strong's G5092), Thanks (εὐχαριστία - Strong's G2169): Expressions of praise and gratitude to God.

- Fall Down (πι□πτω - Strong's G4098): Indicates an act of reverence and submission.

- Worship (προσκυνε□ω - Strong's G4352): Denotes deep adoration and reverence.

- Cast (βα▢λλω - Strong's G906) Crowns (στε▢φανος - Strong's G4735): Symbolizes the relinquishing of their honor and authority in recognition of God's supremacy.

- Worthy (α▢ξιος - Strong's G514): Declares God's deserving nature.

- Created (κτι▢ζω - Strong's G2936): Affirms God's role as the Creator of all things.

The twenty-four elders respond to the worship of the living creatures by falling down before God's throne, casting their crowns, and declaring His worthiness to receive glory, honor, and power. They acknowledge God as the Creator and Sustainer of all things, attributing all existence to His will.

Expository Insights

Examining the text through exhaustive Strong's Concordance reveals deeper meanings and connections:

- βλε▢πω (Strong's G991): Indicates John's attentive and expectant gaze.

- θυ▢ρα (Strong's G2374): Symbolizes access to the divine realm.

- ουρανός (Strong's G3772): Refers to the abode of God.

- φωνη▢ (Strong's G5456): Represents divine communication.

- σα▢λπι

γξ (Strong's G4536): Symbolizes a clear and authoritative call.

- ἀναβαίνω ὧδε (Strong's G305, G5602): An invitation to ascend to the heavenly realm.

- δει□κνυμι (Strong's G1166): Indicates a divine revelation of future events.

- ἐν πνεύματι (Strong's G1722, G4151): Indicates a state of spiritual vision and revelation.

- θρο□νος (Strong's G2362): Represents God's sovereign authority and rule.

- καθη□μαι (Strong's G2521): Denotes a position of authority and judgment.

- ια□σπιδ (Strong's G2393): A precious stone symbolizing purity and majesty.

- σα□ρδιος (Strong's G4555): A reddish stone symbolizing God's fiery judgment and glory.

- ι□ρις (Strong's G2463): Represents God's covenant faithfulness and mercy.

- σμαραγδι□ν (Strong's G4664): A green stone symbolizing life and renewal.

- θα□λασσα υἄλινος (Strong's G2281, G5193): Symbolizes purity, clarity, and peace.

- ζῶον (Strong's G2226): Represents angelic beings or cherubim.

- ὀφθαλμός (Strong's G3788): Symbolize knowledge and vigilance.

- λε□ων (Strong's G3023), μόσχος (Strong's G3448), α□νθρωπος (Strong's G444), ἀετός (Strong's G105): Represent strength, service, intelligence, and swiftness, respectively.

- ε□ξ πτερύγιον (Strong's G1803, G4420): Indicate mobility and readiness to serve.

- α□γιος, α□γιος, α□γιος (Strong's G40): Emphasizes the absolute holiness of God.

- Κυ□ριος Θεο□ς παντοκράτωρ (Strong's G2962, G2316, G3841): Declares God's supreme authority and power.

- ὁ ἠ̃ν και□ ὁ ὡ□ν και□ ὁ ἐρχόμενος (Strong's G1510, G3739, G2064): Affirms God's eternal existence.

- δο□ξα (Strong's G1391), τιμή (Strong's G5092), εὐχαριστία (Strong's G2169): Expressions of praise and gratitude to God.

- πι□πτω (Strong's G4098): Indicates an act of reverence and submission.

- προσκυνε□ω (Strong's G4352): Denotes deep adoration and reverence.

- βα□λλω (Strong's G906) στε□φανος (Strong's G4735): Symbolizes the relinquishing of their honor and authority in recognition of God's supremacy.

- α□ξιος (Strong's G514): Declares God's deserving nature.

- κτι□ζω (Strong's G2936): Affirms God's role as the Creator of all things.

Practical Application

The vision of the throne room in Revelation 4 holds timeless relevance for believers today. Key lessons include:

1. Acknowledging God's Sovereignty: The vision emphasizes God's absolute sovereignty and authority over all creation. Believers are called to recognize and submit to His supreme rule.

2. Engaging in Worship: The continuous worship by the living creatures and the elders highlights the importance of worship in the life of believers. Worship is an acknowledgment of God's holiness, worthiness, and creative power.

3. Living with Spiritual Awareness: The presence of the living creatures, full of eyes, symbolizes vigilance and awareness. Believers are encouraged to live with spiritual insight and attentiveness to God's presence and activity.

4. Embracing Purity and Righteousness: The white garments of the elders and the sea of glass symbolize purity and righteousness. Believers are called to live lives that reflect the holiness and purity of God.

5. Recognizing Jesus' Authority: The vision underscores Jesus' preeminence and authority as the Beginning of the creation of God. Believers are to honor and follow Him as the sovereign Lord.

Conclusion

The vision of the throne room in Revelation 4 provides a profound depiction of God's sovereignty, holiness, and authority. Through the vivid imagery of the throne, the living creatures, and the twenty-four elders, believers are called to acknowledge God's supreme rule, engage in continuous worship, and live with spiritual awareness, purity, and righteousness. By examining these verses through an expository study with exhaustive Strong's Concordance, we uncover the depth of this heavenly vision and its enduring relevance for the church today. As we embrace the truths revealed in this vision, we will be drawn into deeper worship and greater alignment with God's sovereign purposes.

CHAPTER 05

THE LAMB AND THE SCROLL

Revelation 5 presents a profound vision where Jesus is revealed as the Lamb who was slain, the only one worthy to open the sealed scroll. This chapter emphasizes Jesus' redemptive work and His authority to execute God's plan for humanity. By examining these verses through an expository study with exhaustive Strong's Concordance, we can uncover the deeper meanings and profound truths revealed in this vision.

The Scroll and the Search for the Worthy One

Revelation 5:1-4 introduces the sealed scroll and the search for someone worthy to open it:

> "And I saw in the right hand of Him who sat on the throne a scroll written inside and on the back, sealed with seven seals. Then I saw a strong angel proclaiming with a loud voice, 'Who is worthy to open the scroll and to loose its seals?' And no one in heaven or on the earth or under the earth was able to open the scroll, or to look at it. So I wept much,

because no one was found worthy to open and read the scroll, or to look at it."

- Right Hand (δεξια□ - Strong's G1188): Symbolizes power and authority.

- Scroll (βιβλι□ον - Strong's G975): Represents God's revealed will and plan.

- Sealed with Seven Seals (σφραγι□ς επτα□ - Strong's G4973, G2033): Indicates completeness and divine protection.

- Strong Angel (α□γγελος ἰσχυρός - Strong's G32, G2478): Represents a powerful messenger of God.

- Worthy (α□ξιος - Strong's G514): Signifies being deserving or having the right to act.

- Wept Much (κλαι□ω πολυ□ς - Strong's G2799, G4183): Expresses deep sorrow and lamentation.

The sealed scroll in God's right hand symbolizes His sovereign plan, written inside and out, indicating its thoroughness and completeness. The strong angel's proclamation and the subsequent search emphasize the gravity of finding someone worthy to open the scroll, leading to John's profound sorrow when no one is found.

The Revelation of the Lamb

Revelation 5:5-7 reveals Jesus as the worthy Lamb:

> "But one of the elders said to me, 'Do not weep. Behold, the Lion of the tribe of Judah, the Root of David, has prevailed to open the scroll and to loose its seven seals.' And I looked, and behold, in the midst of the throne and of the four living creatures, and in the midst of the elders, stood a Lamb as though it had been slain, having seven horns and seven eyes, which are the seven Spirits of God sent out into all the earth. Then He came and took the scroll out of the right hand of Him who sat on the throne."

- Elder (πρεσβύτερος - Strong's G4245): Represents mature and authoritative figures in the heavenly realm.

- Lion of the Tribe of Judah (λεῶν φυλή Ἰούδα - Strong's G3023, G5443, G2455): Symbolizes Jesus' kingship and messianic authority (Genesis 49:9-10).

- Root of David (ῥίζα Δαυίδ - Strong's G4491, G1138): Emphasizes Jesus' fulfillment of Davidic lineage prophecies (Isaiah 11:1, 10).

- Lamb (ἀρνίον - Strong's G721): Represents Jesus as the sacrificial Lamb who takes away the sins of the world (John 1:29).

- Slain (σφάζω - Strong's G4969): Indicates Jesus' sacrificial death.

- Seven Horns (κέρας επτά - Strong's G2768, G2033): Symbolizes complete power and authority.

- Seven Eyes (ὀφθαλμός ἐπτά - Strong's G3788, G2033): Represents complete knowledge and the seven Spirits of God.

- Took (λαμβάνω - Strong's G2983): Signifies Jesus' authority and action.

The elder's assurance and the vision of the Lamb reveal Jesus' dual identity as both the conquering Lion and the sacrificial Lamb. His seven horns and seven eyes symbolize His complete power and knowledge, and His ability to take the scroll signifies His authority to execute God's plan.

The Worship of the Lamb

Revelation 5:8-10 describes the worship offered to the Lamb:

> "Now when He had taken the scroll, the four living creatures and the twenty-four elders fell down before the Lamb, each having a harp, and golden bowls full of incense, which are the prayers of the saints. And they sang a new song, saying: 'You are worthy to take the scroll, And to open its seals; For You were slain, And have redeemed us to God by Your blood Out of every tribe and tongue and people and nation, And have made us kings and priests to our God; And we shall reign on the earth.'"

- Fell Down (πι□πτω - Strong's G4098): Indicates an act of reverence and submission.

- Harp (κιθα□ρα - Strong's G2788): Symbolizes worship and praise.

- Golden Bowls of Incense (φια□λη χρυσοῦς θυμίαμα - Strong's G5357, G5552, G2368): Represents the prayers of the saints.

- New Song (καινο□ς ᾠδή - Strong's G2537, G5603): Indicates a fresh, divinely inspired song of praise.

- Redeemed (ἀγοράζω - Strong's G59): Refers to being bought back or ransomed.

- Kings and Priests (βασιλευ□ς και□ ἱερεύς - Strong's G935, G2409): Indicates a royal and priestly status.

The worship of the Lamb involves profound acts of reverence, with the living creatures and elders falling down before Him, each holding a harp and golden bowls of incense. The new song they sing celebrates Jesus' worthiness, His redemptive sacrifice, and the believers' new status as kings and priests.

The Heavenly Proclamation

Revelation 5:11-12 describes the broader heavenly response to the Lamb:

> "Then I looked, and I heard the voice of many angels around the throne, the living creatures, and the elders;

and the number of them was ten thousand times ten thousand, and thousands of thousands, saying with a loud voice: 'Worthy is the Lamb who was slain To receive power and riches and wisdom, And strength and honor and glory and blessing!'"

- Voice (φωνη□ - Strong's G5456): Represents a collective proclamation.

- Many Angels (πολυ□ς α□γγελος - Strong's G4183, G32): Indicates a vast, innumerable host of angels.

- Loud Voice (με□γας φωνη□ - Strong's G3173, G5456): Symbolizes the intensity and magnitude of their praise.

- Worthy (α□ξιος - Strong's G514): Declares the Lamb's deserving nature.

- Power (δυ□ναμις - Strong's G1411), Riches (πλοῦτος - Strong's G4149), Wisdom (σοφία - Strong's G4678), Strength (ἰσχὺς - Strong's G2479), Honor (τιμή - Strong's G5092), Glory (δόξα - Strong's G1391), Blessing (ευλογία - Strong's G2129): Attributes and praises ascribed to the Lamb.

The vision expands to include a vast multitude of angels, living creatures, and elders, all proclaiming the worthiness of the Lamb. Their collective voice magnifies Jesus' worthiness to receive all power, riches, wisdom, strength, honor, glory, and blessing.

The Universal Worship

Revelation 5:13-14 concludes with a universal act of worship:

> "And every creature which is in heaven and on the earth and under the earth and such as are in the sea, and all that are in them, I heard saying: 'Blessing and honor and glory and power Be to Him who sits on the throne, And to the Lamb, forever and ever!' Then the four living creatures said, 'Amen!' And the twenty-four elders fell down and worshiped Him who lives forever and ever."

- Every Creature (πᾶς κτίσμα - Strong's G3956, G2937): Indicates the inclusivity of all creation.

- Blessing (εὐλογία - Strong's G2129), Honor (τιμή - Strong's G5092), Glory (δόξα - Strong's G1391), Power (κράτος - Strong's G2904): Attributes of praise ascribed to God and the Lamb.

- Forever and Ever (εἰς του☐ς αἰῶνας τῶν αἰώνων - Strong's G1519, G3588, G165, G3588, G165): Emphasizes the eternal nature of the praise.

- Amen (Αμη☐ν - Strong's G281): An affirmation of truth and agreement.

The final vision encompasses every creature in heaven, on earth, under the earth, and in the sea, all joining in a universal declaration of praise to God and the Lamb. The living creatures affirm with "Amen," and the elders fall down and worship, completing the scene of universal and eternal worship.

Expository Insights

Examining the text through exhaustive Strong's Concordance reveals deeper meanings and connections:

- δεξια□ (Strong's G1188): Symbolizes power and authority.

- βιβλι□ον (Strong's G975): Represents God's revealed will and plan.

- σφραγι□ς επτα□ (Strong's G4973, G2033): Indicates completeness and divine protection.

- α□γγελος ἰσχυρός (Strong's G32, G2478): Represents a powerful messenger of God.

- α□ξιος (Strong's G514): Signifies being deserving or having the right to act.

- κλαι□ω πολυ□ς (Strong's G2799, G4183): Expresses deep sorrow and lamentation.

- πρεσβυ□τερος (Strong's G4245): Represents mature and authoritative figures in the heavenly realm.

- λε□ων φυλή Ἰούδα (Strong's G3023, G5443, G2455): Symbolizes Jesus' kingship and messianic authority.

- ῥίζα Δαυίδ (Strong's G4491, G1138): Emphasizes Jesus' fulfillment of Davidic lineage prophecies.

- ἀρνίον (Strong's G721): Represents Jesus as the sacrificial Lamb who takes away the sins of the world.

- σφα□ζω (Strong's G4969): Indicates Jesus' sacrificial death.

- κε□ρας επτα□ (Strong's G2768, G2033): Symbolizes complete power and authority.

- ὀφθαλμός επτά (Strong's G3788, G2033): Represents complete knowledge and the seven Spirits of God.

- λαμβα□νω (Strong's G2983): Signifies Jesus' authority and action.

- πι□πτω (Strong's G4098): Indicates an act of reverence and submission.

- κιθα□ρα (Strong's G2788): Symbolizes worship and praise.

- φια□λη χρυσοῦς θυμίαμα (Strong's G5357, G5552, G2368): Represents the prayers of the saints.

- καινο□ς ᾠδή (Strong's G2537, G5603): Indicates a fresh, divinely inspired song of praise.

- ἀγοράζω (Strong's G59): Refers to being bought back or ransomed.

- βασιλευ□ς και□ ἱερεύς (Strong's G935, G2409): Indicates a royal and priestly status.

- φωνη□ (Strong's G5456): Represents a collective proclamation.

- πολυ☐ ς α☐ γγελος (Strong's G4183, G32): Indicates a vast, innumerable host of angels.

- με☐ γας φωνη☐ (Strong's G3173, G5456): Symbolizes the intensity and magnitude of their praise.

- δυ☐ ναμις (Strong's G1411), πλοῦτος (Strong's G4149), σοφία (Strong's G4678), ἰσχύς (Strong's G2479), τιμή (Strong's G5092), δόξα (Strong's G1391), ευλογία (Strong's G2129): Attributes and praises ascribed to the Lamb.

- πᾶς κτίσμα (Strong's G3956, G2937): Indicates the inclusivity of all creation.

- ευλογία (Strong's G2129), τιμή (Strong's G5092), δόξα (Strong's G1391), κράτος (Strong's G2904): Attributes of praise ascribed to God and the Lamb.

- εἰς του☐ ς αἰῶνας τῶν αἰώνων (Strong's G1519, G3588, G165, G3588, G165): Emphasizes the eternal nature of the praise.

- Αμη☐ ν (Strong's G281): An affirmation of truth and agreement.

Practical Application

The vision of the Lamb and the scroll in Revelation 5 holds timeless relevance for believers today. Key lessons include:

1. Acknowledging Jesus' Worthiness: Jesus is the only one worthy to open the scroll and execute God's plan.

Believers are called to recognize and honor His unique worthiness and authority.

2. Understanding Jesus' Redemptive Work: The imagery of the Lamb who was slain emphasizes Jesus' sacrificial death and redemptive work. Believers are reminded of the profound significance of His sacrifice.

3. Engaging in Worship: The worship of the Lamb by the heavenly beings highlights the importance of worship in the life of believers. Worship is an acknowledgment of Jesus' worthiness and redemptive work.

4. Living as Kings and Priests: Believers are redeemed to be kings and priests to God, signifying a royal and priestly status. This calls for a life of service, worship, and dedication to God's purposes.

5. Joining the Universal Praise: The universal worship of God and the Lamb by all creation underscores the inclusivity of praise. Believers are encouraged to join in this eternal and universal act of worship.

Conclusion

The vision of the Lamb and the scroll in Revelation 5 provides a profound depiction of Jesus' worthiness, redemptive work, and authority. Through the imagery of the Lamb who was slain and the worship offered by heavenly beings and all creation, believers are called to acknowledge

Jesus' unique worthiness, engage in worship, and live as kings and priests to God. By examining these verses through an expository study with exhaustive Strong's Concordance, we uncover the depth of this heavenly vision and its enduring relevance for the church today. As we embrace the truths revealed in this vision, we will be drawn into deeper worship and greater alignment with God's redemptive purposes.

CHAPTER 06

THE SEVEN SEALS

Revelation 6-8 describes the opening of the seven seals, revealing a series of judgments and events that lead up to the end times. These seals emphasize Jesus' control over history and His role in bringing about God's ultimate plan for justice and redemption. By examining these verses through an expository study with exhaustive Strong's Concordance, we can uncover the deeper meanings and significant truths revealed in this vision.

The First Seal: The Conqueror

Revelation 6:1-2 describes the opening of the first seal:

> "Now I saw when the Lamb opened one of the seals; and I heard one of the four living creatures saying with a voice like thunder, 'Come and see.' And I looked, and behold, a white horse. He who sat on it had a bow; and a crown was given to him, and he went out conquering and to conquer."

- Lamb (ἀρνίον - Strong's G721): Refers to Jesus Christ as the sacrificial Lamb.

- Seal (σφραγι□ς - Strong's G4973): Represents a mark of authority and revelation.

- Living Creatures (ζῶον - Strong's G2226): Symbolizes angelic beings or cherubim.

- White Horse (λευκο□ς □ππος - Strong's G3022, G2462): Represents conquest and victory.

- Bow (το□ξον - Strong's G5115): Symbolizes military power and strength.

- Crown (στε□φανος - Strong's G4735): Represents victory and authority.

- Conquering and to Conquer (νικα□ω - Strong's G3528): Indicates continuous victory and dominion.

The opening of the first seal reveals a rider on a white horse, symbolizing conquest and victory. This rider, given a crown, represents a force of power and authority going forth to conquer.

The Second Seal: Conflict on Earth

Revelation 6:3-4 describes the opening of the second seal:

> "When He opened the second seal, I heard the second living creature saying, 'Come and see.' Another horse, fiery red, went out. And it was granted to the one who sat on

it to take peace from the earth, and that people should kill one another; and there was given to him a great sword."

- Fiery Red Horse (πυῤῥὸς ἵππος - Strong's G4450, G2462): Represents war and bloodshed.

- Peace (εἰρήνη - Strong's G1515): Symbolizes harmony and absence of conflict.

- Kill (σφάζω - Strong's G4969): Indicates slaughter and violence.

- Great Sword (μάχαιρα μεγάλη - Strong's G3162, G3173): Represents extensive warfare and destruction.

The second seal reveals a rider on a fiery red horse, symbolizing conflict and bloodshed. This rider is granted the power to take peace from the earth, leading to widespread violence and war.

The Third Seal: Scarcity on Earth

Revelation 6:5-6 describes the opening of the third seal:

> "When He opened the third seal, I heard the third living creature say, 'Come and see.' So I looked, and behold, a black horse, and he who sat on it had a pair of scales in his hand. And I heard a voice in the midst of the four living creatures saying, 'A quart of wheat for a denarius, and three quarts of barley for a denarius; and do not harm the oil and the wine.'"

- Black Horse (με□λας □ππος - Strong's G3189, G2462): Represents famine and scarcity.

- Pair of Scales (ζυγο□ς - Strong's G2218): Symbolizes measurement and rationing.

- Quart of Wheat (χοῖνιξ σῖτος - Strong's G5518, G4621): Represents a small measure of food.

- Denarius (δηνα□ριον - Strong's G1220): Represents a day's wage.

- Barley (κριθη□ - Strong's G2915): Represents a cheaper grain.

- Oil and Wine (ε□λαιον και□ οἶνος - Strong's G1637, G3631): Represents basic necessities.

The third seal reveals a rider on a black horse, symbolizing famine and economic hardship. The pair of scales represents rationing, and the voice describes exorbitant prices for basic food items, indicating severe scarcity.

The Fourth Seal: Widespread Death

Revelation 6:7-8 describes the opening of the fourth seal:

> "When He opened the fourth seal, I heard the voice of the fourth living creature saying, 'Come and see.' So I looked, and behold, a pale horse. And the name of him who sat on it was Death, and Hades followed with him. And power was given to them over a fourth of the earth, to kill with

sword, with hunger, with death, and by the beasts of the earth."

- Pale Horse (χλωρο☐ς ☐ππος - Strong's G5515, G2462): Represents death and decay.

- Death (θα☐νατος - Strong's G2288): Personifies mortality and the end of life.

- Hades (α☐δης - Strong's G86): Represents the realm of the dead.

- Sword (μα☐χαιρα - Strong's G3162), Hunger (λιμο☐ς - Strong's G3042), Death (θα☐νατος - Strong's G2288), Beasts (θηρι☐ον - Strong's G2342): Instruments of widespread death and destruction.

The fourth seal reveals a rider on a pale horse, symbolizing death, accompanied by Hades. This rider is given power over a fourth of the earth, bringing death through various means, including warfare, famine, plague, and wild animals.

The Fifth Seal: The Cry of the Martyrs

Revelation 6:9-11 describes the opening of the fifth seal:

> "When He opened the fifth seal, I saw under the altar the souls of those who had been slain for the word of God and for the testimony which they held. And they cried with a loud voice, saying, 'How long, O Lord, holy and true,

until You judge and avenge our blood on those who dwell on the earth?' Then a white robe was given to each of them; and it was said to them that they should rest a little while longer, until both the number of their fellow servants and their brethren, who would be killed as they were, was completed."

- Altar (θυσιαστη□ριον - Strong's G2379): Represents the place of sacrifice and divine presence.

- Souls (ψυχη□ - Strong's G5590): Represents the immaterial essence of the martyrs.

- Slain (σφα□ζω - Strong's G4969): Indicates their martyrdom for their faith.

- Word of God (λο□γος τοῦ Θεοῦ - Strong's G3056, G2316): Represents the divine message and truth.

- Testimony (μαρτυρι□α - Strong's G3141): Refers to their witness and confession of faith.

- White Robe (λευκο□ς στολή - Strong's G3022, G4749): Symbolizes purity and victory.

- Rest (ἀναπαύω - Strong's G373): Indicates a period of waiting and repose.

The fifth seal reveals the souls of the martyrs under the altar, crying out for justice and vindication. They are given white robes and told to rest a little longer until the full number of their fellow martyrs is completed.

The Sixth Seal: Cosmic Disturbances

Revelation 6:12-17 describes the opening of the sixth seal:

> "I looked when He opened the sixth seal, and behold, there was a great earthquake; and the sun became black as sackcloth of hair, and the moon became like blood. And the stars of heaven fell to the earth, as a fig tree drops its late figs when it is shaken by a mighty wind. Then the sky receded as a scroll when it is rolled up, and every mountain and island was moved out of its place. And the kings of the earth, the great men, the rich men, the commanders, the mighty men, every slave and every free man, hid themselves in the caves and in the rocks of the mountains, and said to the mountains and rocks, 'Fall on us and hide us from the face of Him who sits on the throne and from the wrath of the Lamb! For the great day of His wrath has come, and who is able to stand?'"

- Great Earthquake (σεισμο□ς μεγάς - Strong's G4578, G3173): Represents a significant seismic event.

- Sun (η□λιος - Strong's G2246): Represents the primary source of light.

- Black as Sackcloth (με□λας σα□κκος - Strong's G3189, G4526): Indicates darkness and mourning.

- Moon (σελη□νη - Strong's

G4582): Represents the secondary source of light.

- Blood (αἷμα - Strong's G129): Symbolizes ominous signs and judgment.

- Stars (ἀστήρ - Strong's G792): Represents celestial bodies.

- Sky (οὐρανός - Strong's G3772): Refers to the visible heavens.

- Scroll (βιβλι□ον - Strong's G975): Represents a rolled-up document.

- Mountains and Islands (ο□ ρος και□ νῆσος - Strong's G3735, G3520): Symbolize stable landforms.

- Wrath (ὀργή - Strong's G3709): Indicates divine judgment and anger.

The sixth seal reveals cosmic disturbances, including a great earthquake, darkening of the sun and moon, falling stars, and the receding sky. These cataclysmic events lead to widespread fear and panic, as people recognize the impending wrath of God and the Lamb.

The Interlude: The Sealing of the 144,000

Revelation 7:1-8 describes the sealing of the 144,000:

> "After these things I saw four angels standing at the four corners of the earth, holding the four winds of the earth, that the wind should not blow on the earth, on the sea, or on any tree. Then I saw another angel ascending from the east, having the seal of the living God. And he cried with a loud

voice to the four angels to whom it was granted to harm the earth and the sea, saying, 'Do not harm the earth, the sea, or the trees till we have sealed the servants of our God on their foreheads.' And I heard the number of those who were sealed. One hundred and forty-four thousand of all the tribes of the children of Israel were sealed."

- Four Angels (τε□ σσαρες α□ γγελος - Strong's G5064, G32): Represents angels at the four corners of the earth.

- Four Corners (τε□ σσαρες γωνι□ α - Strong's G5064, G1137): Symbolizes the entirety of the earth.

- Winds (α□ νεμος - Strong's G417): Represents destructive forces.

- Seal of the Living God (σφραγι□ ς ζῶν Θεός - Strong's G4973, G2198, G2316): Indicates divine protection and ownership.

- Servants (δοῦλος - Strong's G1401): Refers to God's faithful followers.

- Foreheads (με□ τωπον - Strong's G3359): Symbolizes the visible mark of God's ownership.

Before the seventh seal is opened, an interlude describes the sealing of 144,000 servants of God, representing protection and divine ownership.

The Seventh Seal: Silence in Heaven

Revelation 8:1-2 describes the opening of the seventh seal:

> "When He opened the seventh seal, there was silence in heaven for about half an hour. And I saw the seven angels who stand before God, and to them were given seven trumpets."

- Silence (σιγη□ - Strong's G4602): Represents a solemn pause and anticipation.

- Half an Hour (ἡμιώριον - Strong's G2256): Indicates a specific, brief period.

- Seven Angels (ἑπτα□ α□γγελος - Strong's G2033, G32): Refers to seven specific angels before God.

- Seven Trumpets (ἑπτα□ σάλπιγξ - Strong's G2033, G4536): Symbolizes forthcoming judgments and announcements.

The opening of the seventh seal results in a profound silence in heaven, followed by the preparation of seven angels with seven trumpets, signaling the next series of judgments.

Expository Insights

Examining the text through exhaustive Strong's Concordance reveals deeper meanings and connections:

- ἀρνίον (Strong's G721): Refers to Jesus Christ as the sacrificial Lamb.

- σφραγι□ς (Strong's G4973): Represents a mark of authority and revelation.

- ζῶον (Strong's G2226): Symbolizes angelic beings or cherubim.

- λευκο□ς □ππος (Strong's G3022, G2462): Represents conquest and victory.

- το□ ξον (Strong's G5115): Symbolizes military power and strength.

- στε□ φανος (Strong's G4735): Represents victory and authority.

- νικα□ ω (Strong's G3528): Indicates continuous victory and dominion.

- πυρρὸς □ ππος (Strong's G4450, G2462): Represents war and bloodshed.

- εἰρήνη (Strong's G1515): Symbolizes harmony and absence of conflict.

- σφα□ ζω (Strong's G4969): Indicates slaughter and violence.

- μα□ χαιρα μεγα□ λη (Strong's G3162, G3173): Represents extensive warfare and destruction.

- με□ λας □ππος (Strong's G3189, G2462): Represents famine and scarcity.

- ζυγο□ ς (Strong's G2218): Symbolizes measurement and rationing.

- χοῖνιξ σῖτος (Strong's G5518, G4621): Represents a small measure of food.

- δηνα□ριον (Strong's G1220): Represents a day's wage.

- κριθη□ (Strong's G2915): Represents a cheaper grain.

- ἐ□λαιον και□ οἶνος (Strong's G1637, G3631): Represents basic necessities.

- χλωρο□ς ι□ππος (Strong's G5515, G2462): Represents death and decay.

- θα□νατος (Strong's G2288): Personifies mortality and the end of life.

- α□᾿δης (Strong's G86): Represents the realm of the dead.

- μα□χαιρα (Strong's G3162), λιμο□ς (Strong's G3042), θα□νατος (Strong's G2288), θηρι□ον (Strong's G2342): Instruments of widespread death and destruction.

- θυσιαστη□ριον (Strong's G2379): Represents the place of sacrifice and divine presence.

- ψυχη□ (Strong's G5590): Represents the immaterial essence of the martyrs.

- λο□γος του̃ Θεου̃ (Strong's G3056, G2316): Represents the divine message and truth.

- μαρτυρι□α (Strong's G3141): Refers to their witness and confession of faith.

- λευκο□ς στολή (Strong's G3022, G4749): Symbolizes purity and victory.

- ἀναπαύω (Strong's G373): Indicates a period of waiting and repose.

- σεισμο□ς μεγάς (Strong's G4578, G3173): Represents a significant seismic event.

- η□λιος (Strong's G2246): Represents the primary source of light.

- με□λας σα□κκος (Strong's G3189, G4526): Indicates darkness and mourning.

- σελη□νη (Strong's G4582): Represents the secondary source of light.

- αἷμα (Strong's G129): Symbolizes ominous signs and judgment.

- ἀστήρ (Strong's G792): Represents celestial bodies.

- οὐρανός (Strong's G3772): Refers to the visible heavens.

- βιβλι□ον (Strong's G975): Represents a rolled-up document.

- ο□ρος και□ νῆσος (Strong's G3735, G3520): Symbolize stable landforms.

- ὀργή (Strong's G3709): Indicates divine judgment and anger.

- τε□σσαρες α□γγελος (Strong's G5064, G32): Represents angels at the four corners of the earth.

- τε□σσαρες γωνι□α (Strong's G5064, G1137): Symbolizes the entirety of the earth.

- α□νεμος (Strong's G417): Represents destructive forces.

- σφραγι□ς ζω̃ν Θεός (Strong's G4973, G2198, G2316): Indicates divine protection and ownership.

- δοὺλος (Strong's G1401): Refers to God's faithful followers.

- με□τωπον (Strong's G3359): Symbolizes the visible mark of God's ownership.

- σιγη□ (Strong's G4602): Represents a solemn pause and anticipation.

- ἡμιώριον (Strong's G2256): Indicates a specific, brief period.

- ε῾πτα□ α□γγελος (Strong's G2033, G32): Refers to seven specific angels before God.

- ἑπτα□ σάλπιγξ (Strong's G2033, G4536): Symbolizes forthcoming judgments and announcements.

Practical Application

The vision of the seven seals in Revelation 6-8 holds timeless relevance for believers today. Key lessons include:

1. Recognizing Jesus' Sovereignty: The opening of the seals by the Lamb emphasizes Jesus' control over history and His authority to execute God's plan. Believers are called to trust in His sovereign rule.

2. Understanding Divine Judgment: The judgments revealed in the seals highlight the reality of God's justice. Believers are reminded of the seriousness of sin and the certainty of divine judgment.

3. Enduring Persecution: The cry of the martyrs under the fifth seal encourages believers to remain faithful even unto death, knowing that God will ultimately vindicate His people.

4. Anticipating Cosmic Signs: The cosmic disturbances associated with the sixth seal remind believers to be watchful and prepared for the significant events that will accompany the end times.

5. Receiving Divine Protection: The sealing of the 144,000 indicates God's protection over His faithful servants. Believers can find assurance in God's care and preservation.

6. Responding to Silence and Anticipation: The silence in heaven at the opening of the seventh seal calls for a solemn and reflective response, recognizing the gravity of the

unfolding events and the anticipation of God's further actions.

Conclusion

The vision of the seven seals in Revelation 6-8 provides a profound depiction of Jesus' authority, divine judgment, and the unfolding of God's plan for the end times. Through the imagery of conquest, conflict, scarcity, death, martyrdom, cosmic disturbances, and divine protection, believers are called to recognize Jesus' sovereignty, understand the seriousness of divine judgment, endure persecution, and anticipate the significant events of the end times. By examining these verses through an expository study with exhaustive Strong's Concordance, we uncover the depth of this vision and its enduring relevance for the church today. As we embrace the truths revealed in the opening of the seven seals, we will be drawn into deeper trust in Jesus' sovereignty and greater readiness for His return.

CHAPTER 07

THE SEVEN TRUMPETS

Revelation 8-11 describes the sounding of the seven trumpets, which bring forth further judgments upon the earth. These events highlight Jesus' authority to judge and His commitment to restoring righteousness. By examining these verses through an expository study with exhaustive Strong's Concordance, we can uncover the deeper meanings and significant truths revealed in this vision.

The First Trumpet: Hail and Fire

Revelation 8:7 describes the sounding of the first trumpet:

> "The first angel sounded: And hail and fire followed, mingled with blood, and they were thrown to the earth. And a third of the trees were burned up, and all green grass was burned up."

- First Angel (πρῶτος α□γγελος - Strong's G4413, G32): Represents the initial messenger of judgment.

- Trumpet (σα□λπιγξ - Strong's G4536): Symbolizes a call to judgment or action.

- Hail and Fire (χάλαζα καὶ πῦρ - Strong's G5464, G2532, G4442): Represents a devastating combination of natural elements.

- Blood (αἷμα - Strong's G129): Indicates destruction and death.

- Third (τρίτος - Strong's G5154): Represents a significant, but partial, measure of judgment.

The first trumpet brings hail and fire mixed with blood, resulting in the destruction of a third of the trees and all green grass. This judgment affects the earth's vegetation, highlighting the severity and scope of divine judgment.

The Second Trumpet: The Burning Mountain

Revelation 8:8-9 describes the sounding of the second trumpet:

> "Then the second angel sounded: And something like a great mountain burning with fire was thrown into the sea, and a third of the sea became blood. And a third of the living creatures in the sea died, and a third of the ships were destroyed."

- Second Angel (δεύτερος ἄγγελος - Strong's G1208, G32): Represents the second messenger of judgment.

- Mountain (ὄρος - Strong's G3735): Symbolizes a significant and imposing element.

- Sea (θα□λασσα - Strong's G2281): Represents the world's oceans and large bodies of water.

- Blood (αἷμα - Strong's G129): Indicates widespread death and destruction.

The second trumpet brings a great burning mountain cast into the sea, resulting in a third of the sea turning to blood, the death of a third of sea creatures, and the destruction of a third of the ships. This judgment impacts the marine ecosystem and commerce.

The Third Trumpet: The Star Wormwood

Revelation 8:10-11 describes the sounding of the third trumpet:

> "Then the third angel sounded: And a great star fell from heaven, burning like a torch, and it fell on a third of the rivers and on the springs of water. The name of the star is Wormwood. A third of the waters became wormwood, and many men died from the water, because it was made bitter."

- Third Angel (τρι□τος α□γγελος - Strong's G5154, G32): Represents the third messenger of judgment.

- Great Star (με□γας ἀστήρ - Strong's G3173, G792): Symbolizes a celestial object of significant impact.

- Wormwood (α□ψινθος - Strong's G894): Represents bitterness and poison.

- Rivers and Springs (ποταμο□ς και□ πηγή - Strong's G4215, G4077): Indicates fresh water sources.

The third trumpet brings a great burning star, named Wormwood, falling from heaven and contaminating a third of the rivers and springs of water. The waters become bitter, resulting in the death of many people. This judgment affects the earth's fresh water supply.

The Fourth Trumpet: Darkness

Revelation 8:12 describes the sounding of the fourth trumpet:

> "Then the fourth angel sounded: And a third of the sun was struck, a third of the moon, and a third of the stars, so that a third of them were darkened. A third of the day did not shine, and likewise the night."

- Fourth Angel (τε□ταρτος α□γγελος - Strong's G5067, G32): Represents the fourth messenger of judgment.

- Sun, Moon, and Stars (η□λιος, σελήνη, ἀστήρ - Strong's G2246, G4582, G792): Represent the primary sources of light for the earth.

- Darkened (σκοτι□ζω - Strong's G4654): Indicates a reduction in light and visibility.

The fourth trumpet brings darkness upon a third of the sun, moon, and stars, resulting in diminished light during both day and night. This judgment affects the natural order and rhythm of day and night.

The Eagle's Woe

Revelation 8:13 introduces a warning of intensified judgments:

> "And I looked, and I heard an angel flying through the midst of heaven, saying with a loud voice, 'Woe, woe, woe to the inhabitants of the earth, because of the remaining blasts of the trumpet of the three angels who are about to sound!'"

- Angel (α□γγελος - Strong's G32): Represents a messenger of warning.

- Woe (οὐαί - Strong's G3759): Indicates great sorrow or distress.

The angel's proclamation of three woes emphasizes the increasing severity of the judgments to come with the next three trumpets.

The Fifth Trumpet: The Locusts from the Abyss

Revelation 9:1-12 describes the sounding of the fifth trumpet:

> "Then the fifth angel sounded: And I saw a star fallen from heaven to the earth. To him was given the key to the bottomless pit. And he opened the bottomless pit, and smoke arose out of the pit like the smoke of a great furnace. So the sun and the air were darkened because of the smoke of

the pit. Then out of the smoke locusts came upon the earth. And to them was given power, as the scorpions of the earth have power. They were commanded not to harm the grass of the earth, or any green thing, or any tree, but only those men who do not have the seal of God on their foreheads. And they were not given authority to kill them, but to torment them for five months. Their torment was like the torment of a scorpion when it strikes a man. In those days men will seek death and will not find it; they will desire to die, and death will flee from them."

- Star (ἀστήρ - Strong's G792): Represents a fallen angelic being.

- Bottomless Pit (ἄβυσσος - Strong's G12): Represents the abyss or the underworld.

- Locusts (ἀκρίς - Strong's G200): Symbolizes a plague of destructive creatures.

- Seal of God (σφραγὶς Θεοῦς - Strong's G4973, G2316): Indicates divine protection and ownership.

The fifth trumpet brings a star fallen from heaven, given the key to the bottomless pit. When the pit is opened, smoke and locusts emerge, tormenting those who do not have the seal of God. This torment lasts for five months, causing intense suffering without death.

The Sixth Trumpet: The Release of the Four Angels

Revelation 9:13-21 describes the sounding of the sixth trumpet:

> "Then the sixth angel sounded: And I heard a voice from the four horns of the golden altar which is before God, saying to the sixth angel who had the trumpet, 'Release the four angels who are bound at the great river Euphrates.' So the four angels, who had been prepared for the hour and day and month and year, were released to kill a third of mankind. Now the number of the army of the horsemen was two hundred million; I heard the number of them. And thus I saw the horses in the vision: those who sat on them had breastplates of fiery red, hyacinth blue, and sulfur yellow; and the heads of the horses were like the heads of lions; and out of their mouths came fire, smoke, and brimstone. By these three plagues a third of mankind was killed—by the fire and the smoke and the brimstone which came out of their mouths. For their power is in their mouth and in their tails; for their tails are like serpents, having heads; and with them they do harm."

- Four Angels (τε□σσαρες α□γγελος - Strong's G5064, G32): Represents angelic beings prepared for judgment.

- Euphrates (Εὐφράτης - Strong's G2166): Represents a significant river often associated with boundary and judgment.

- Third (τρι□τος - Strong's G5154): Represents a significant, but partial, measure of judgment.

- Army of Horsemen (στρατευ□μα ι□ππος - Strong's G4753, G2462): Symbolizes a vast and formidable force.

The sixth trumpet releases four bound angels at the Euphrates, leading an army of two hundred million horsemen. These horsemen bring plagues of fire, smoke, and brimstone, resulting in the death of a third of mankind. This judgment brings widespread destruction and emphasizes the severity of divine wrath.

The Interlude: The Mighty Angel with the Little Book Revelation 10 describes an interlude before the seventh trumpet:

> "I saw still another mighty angel coming down from heaven, clothed with a cloud. And a rainbow was on his head, his face was like the sun, and his feet like pillars of fire. He had a little book open in his hand. And he set his right foot on the sea and his left foot on the land, and cried with a loud voice, as when a lion roars. When he cried out, seven thunders uttered their voices."

- Mighty Angel (ἰσχυρός α□γγελος - Strong's G2478, G32): Represents a powerful messenger of God.

- Little Book (βιβλαρι□διον - Strong's G974): Symbolizes a specific divine revelation.

This interlude features a mighty angel with a little book, standing on both the sea and the land, and crying out with a loud voice. The seven thunders respond, indicating further revelation and judgment.

The Seventh Trumpet: The Kingdom Proclaimed

Revelation 11:15-19 describes the sounding of the seventh trumpet:

> "Then the seventh angel sounded: And there were loud voices in heaven, saying, 'The kingdoms of this world have become the kingdoms of our Lord and of His Christ, and He shall reign forever and ever!' And the twenty-four elders who sat before God on their thrones fell on their faces and worshiped God, saying: 'We give You thanks, O Lord God Almighty, The One who is and who was and who is to come, Because You have taken Your great power and reigned. The nations were angry, and Your wrath has come, And the time of the dead, that they should be judged, And that You should reward Your servants the prophets and the saints, And those who fear Your name, small and great, And should destroy those who destroy the earth.' Then the temple of God was opened in heaven, and the ark of His covenant was seen in His temple. And there were lightnings, noises, thunderings, an earthquake, and great hail."

- Seventh Angel (ἕ□βδομος ἄ□γγελος - Strong's G1442, G32): Represents the final messenger of judgment.

- Kingdoms of This World (βασιλεἰ□α τοῦ κόσμος - Strong's G932, G2889): Represents the earthly dominions.

- Reign Forever (βασιλεύω εἰς τοὺς αἰῶνας - Strong's G936, G1519, G3588, G165): Indicates eternal dominion.

- Wrath (ὀργή - Strong's G3709): Indicates divine judgment.

- Temple of God (ναο□ς τοῦ Θεοῦ - Strong's G3485, G2316): Represents the divine sanctuary.

- Ark of His Covenant (κιβωτο□ς διαθήκη - Strong's G2787, G1242): Symbolizes God's faithfulness and promises.

The seventh trumpet proclaims the establishment of God's eternal kingdom, with loud voices in heaven declaring the reign of the Lord and His Christ. The twenty-four elders worship God, acknowledging His power and justice. The opening of the temple in heaven and the appearance of the ark of His covenant signify the fulfillment of God's promises and the commencement of final judgment.

Expository Insights

Examining the text through exhaustive Strong's Concordance reveals deeper meanings and connections:

- πρῶτος ἄ□γγελος (Strong's G4413, G32): Represents the initial messenger of judgment.

- σα□λπιγξ (Strong's G4536): Symbolizes a call to judgment or action.

- χα□λαζα καί□ πῦρ (Strong's G5464, G2532, G4442): Represents a devastating combination of natural elements.

- αἷμα (Strong's G129): Indicates destruction and death.

- τρί□τος (Strong's G5154): Represents a significant, but partial, measure of judgment.

- δεύ□τερος α□γγελος (Strong's G1208, G32): Represents the second messenger of judgment.

- ο□ρος (Strong's G3735): Symbolizes a significant and imposing element.

- θα□λασσα (Strong's G2281): Represents the world's oceans and large bodies of water.

- τρί□τος (Strong's G5154): Represents a significant, but partial, measure of judgment.

- τρί□τος α□γγελος (Strong's G5154, G32): Represents the third messenger of judgment.

- μέ□γας ἀστήρ (Strong's G3173, G792): Symbolizes a celestial object of significant impact.

- α□ψινθος (Strong's G894): Represents bitterness and poison.

- ποταμο□ς καί□ πηγή (Strong's G4215, G4077): Indicates fresh water sources.

- τε□ταρτος α□γγελος (Strong's G5067, G32): Represents the fourth messenger of judgment.

- η□λιος, σελήνη, α□στήρ (Strong's G2246, G4582, G792): Represent the primary sources of light for the earth.

- σκοτι□ζω (Strong's G4654): Indicates a reduction in light and visibility.

- α□γγελος (Strong's G32): Represents a messenger of warning.

- ου□αί (Strong's G3759): Indicates great sorrow or distress.

- α□στήρ (Strong's G792): Represents a fallen angelic being.

- α□βυσσος (Strong's G12): Represents the abyss or the underworld.

- α□κρίς (Strong's G200): Symbolizes a plague of destructive creatures.

- σφραγι□ς Θεο□ς (Strong's G4973, G2316): Indicates divine protection and ownership.

- τε□σσαρες α□γγελος (Strong's G5064, G32): Represents angelic beings prepared for judgment.

- Ευ□φράτης (Strong's G2166): Represents a significant river often associated with boundary and judgment.

- στρατευ□μα □ππος (Strong's G4753, G2462): Symbolizes a vast and formidable force.

- ἰσχυρὸς ἀ□γγελος (Strong's G2478, G32): Represents a powerful messenger of God.

- βιβλαρι□διον (Strong's G974): Symbolizes a specific divine revelation.

- ε□βδομος ἀ□γγελος (Strong's G1442, G32): Represents the final messenger of judgment.

- βασιλει□α τοῦ κόσμος (Strong's G932, G2889): Represents the earthly dominions.

- βασιλευ□ω εἰς τοὺς αἰῶνας (Strong's G936, G1519, G3588, G165): Indicates eternal dominion.

- ὀργή (Strong's G3709): Indicates divine judgment.

- ναο□ς τοῦ Θεοῦ (Strong's G3485, G2316): Represents the divine sanctuary.

- κιβωτο□ς διαθήκη (Strong's G2787, G1242): Symbolizes God's faithfulness and promises.

Practical Application

The vision of the seven trumpets in Revelation 8-11 holds timeless relevance for believers today. Key lessons include:

1. Recognizing Jesus' Authority: The sounding of the trumpets by angels emphasizes Jesus' control over judgment and His authority to bring about God's plan. Believers are called to acknowledge and submit to His divine authority.

2. Understanding Divine Judgment: The judgments revealed through the trumpets highlight the reality of God's justice and the seriousness of sin. Believers are reminded of the necessity of repentance and the consequences of unrepentant sin.

3. Enduring Trials and Tribulations: The torments and plagues described in the trumpet judgments call believers to remain steadfast in faith, trusting in God's protection and ultimate deliverance.

4. Anticipating Cosmic Signs: The cosmic disturbances associated with the trumpets remind believers to be watchful and prepared for the significant events that will accompany the end times.

5. Responding to God's Sovereignty: The proclamation of God's eternal kingdom at the seventh trumpet encourages believers to worship and give thanks to God for His sovereign rule and His commitment to restoring righteousness.

Conclusion

The vision of the seven trumpets in Revelation 8-11 provides a profound depiction of Jesus' authority, divine judgment, and the unfolding of God's plan for the end times. Through the imagery of natural disasters, cosmic disturbances, and heavenly proclamations, believers are called to recognize Jesus' sovereignty, understand the seriousness of divine judgment, endure trials, and anticipate the significant events of the end times. By examining these verses through an expository study with exhaustive Strong's Concordance, we uncover the depth of this vision and its enduring relevance for the church today. As we embrace the truths revealed in the sounding of the seven trumpets, we will be drawn into deeper worship and greater readiness for Jesus' return.

CHAPTER 08

THE SEVEN BOWLS OF WRATH

Revelation 15-16 describes the pouring out of the seven bowls of God's wrath, representing the final judgments upon a rebellious world. These judgments demonstrate Jesus' righteous anger against sin and His power to purify creation. By examining these verses through an expository study with exhaustive Strong's Concordance, we can uncover the deeper meanings and significant truths revealed in this vision.

The Prelude to the Bowls

Revelation 15:1-8 sets the stage for the seven bowls:

> "Then I saw another sign in heaven, great and marvelous: seven angels having the seven last plagues, for in them the wrath of God is complete. And I saw something like a sea of glass mingled with fire, and those who have the victory over the beast, over his image and over his mark and over the number of his name, standing on the sea of glass, having harps of God. They sing the song of Moses, the servant of God, and the song of the Lamb, saying: 'Great and marvelous are Your works, Lord God Almighty! Just and true are Your ways, O King of the saints! Who shall not fear You, O Lord, and glorify Your name? For You alone are holy. For

134

all nations shall come and worship before You, for Your judgments have been manifested.' After these things I looked, and behold, the temple of the tabernacle of the testimony in heaven was opened. And out of the temple came the seven angels having the seven plagues, clothed in pure bright linen, and having their chests girded with golden bands. Then one of the four living creatures gave to the seven angels seven golden bowls full of the wrath of God who lives forever and ever. The temple was filled with smoke from the glory of God and from His power, and no one was able to enter the temple till the seven plagues of the seven angels were completed."

- Seven Angels (ἑπτα□ α□γγελος - Strong's G2033, G32): Represent the messengers of the final judgments.

- Seven Last Plagues (ἑπτα□ ἐσχάτος πληγή - Strong's G2033, G2078, G4127): Indicate the completion of God's wrath.

- Wrath (ὀργή - Strong's G3709): Represents divine judgment and anger.

- Sea of Glass (θα□λασσα ὑάλινος - Strong's G2281, G5193): Symbolizes purity and peace mixed with judgment.

- Song of Moses and the Lamb (ᾠδή Μωϋσῆς και□ ὁ ἀρνίον - Strong's G5603, G3475, G2532, G721): Represents the praise of God's deliverance and redemption.

- Temple (ναο□ς - Strong's G3485): Represents the divine sanctuary.

- Smoke (καπνο□ς - Strong's G2586): Symbolizes the presence and glory of God.

The scene in Revelation 15 sets the stage for the pouring out of the bowls, highlighting the finality of God's judgment and the purity and righteousness of His ways.

The First Bowl: Sores on the Wicked

Revelation 16:1-2 describes the pouring out of the first bowl:

> "Then I heard a loud voice from the temple saying to the seven angels, 'Go and pour out the bowls of the wrath of God on the earth.' So the first went and poured out his bowl upon the earth, and a foul and loathsome sore came upon the men who had the mark of the beast and those who worshiped his image."

- Loud Voice (με□γας φωνη□ - Strong's G3173, G5456): Represents a commanding and authoritative voice from the temple.

- Bowl (φια□λη - Strong's G5357): Represents a vessel of divine judgment.

- Wrath of God (ὀργή Θεός - Strong's G3709, G2316): Indicates divine anger and judgment.

- Foul and Loathsome Sore (κακο□ ς και□ πονηρο□ ς ε□ λκος - Strong's G2556, G4190, G1668): Represents painful and grievous afflictions.

- Mark of the Beast (χα□ ραγμα θηρι□ ον - Strong's G5480, G2342): Symbolizes allegiance to the Antichrist.

The first bowl brings painful sores upon those who have the mark of the beast and worship his image, signifying a direct judgment on those who have aligned themselves with evil.

The Second Bowl: Sea Turned to Blood

Revelation 16:3 describes the pouring out of the second bowl:

> "Then the second angel poured out his bowl on the sea, and it became blood as of a dead man; and every living creature in the sea died."

- Sea (θα□ λασσα - Strong's G2281): Represents the world's oceans and large bodies of water.

- Blood (αἷμα - Strong's G129): Indicates widespread death and destruction.

- Living Creature (ψυχη□ ζῶον - Strong's G5590, G2226): Represents marine life.

The second bowl turns the sea into blood, resulting in the death of all marine life. This judgment highlights the severity of God's wrath and its impact on creation.

The Third Bowl: Rivers and Springs Turned to Blood

Revelation 16:4-7 describes the pouring out of the third bowl:

> "Then the third angel poured out his bowl on the rivers and springs of water, and they became blood. And I heard the angel of the waters saying: 'You are righteous, O Lord, the One who is and who was and who is to be, because You have judged these things. For they have shed the blood of saints and prophets, and You have given them blood to drink. For it is their just due.' And I heard another from the altar saying, 'Even so, Lord God Almighty, true and righteous are Your judgments.'"

- Rivers and Springs (ποταμο□ ς και□ πηγή - Strong's G4215, G4077): Represents fresh water sources.

- Blood (αἷμα - Strong's G129): Indicates widespread death and destruction.

- Righteous (δι□καιος - Strong's G1342): Emphasizes God's justice and fairness.

The third bowl turns the rivers and springs into blood, emphasizing the just and righteous nature of God's judgments. This judgment is in response to the shedding of the blood of saints and prophets.

The Fourth Bowl: Scorching Heat

Revelation 16:8-9 describes the pouring out of the fourth bowl:

> "Then the fourth angel poured out his bowl on the sun, and power was given to him to scorch men with fire. And men were scorched with great heat, and they blasphemed the name of God who has power over these plagues; and they did not repent and give Him glory."

- Sun (η□λιος - Strong's G2246): Represents the primary source of light and heat.

- Scorch (καυματι□ζω - Strong's G2739): Indicates severe burning and suffering.

- Blaspheme (βλασφημε□ω - Strong's G987): Represents speaking irreverently or contemptuously about God.

The fourth bowl intensifies the heat of the sun, causing severe scorching and suffering. Despite this, people blaspheme God and refuse to repent, highlighting the hardness of their hearts.

The Fifth Bowl: Darkness and Pain

Revelation 16:10-11 describes the pouring out of the fifth bowl:

> "Then the fifth angel poured out his bowl on the throne of the beast, and his kingdom became full of darkness; and they gnawed their tongues because of the pain. They

blasphemed the God of heaven because of their pains and their sores, and did not repent of their deeds."

- Throne of the Beast (θρο□νος θηρι□ον - Strong's G2362, G2342): Represents the seat of the Antichrist's power.

- Darkness (σκοτο□ς - Strong's G4655): Symbolizes the absence of light and understanding.

- Pain (πο□νος - Strong's G4192): Indicates severe suffering and distress.

The fifth bowl brings darkness and intense pain upon the kingdom of the beast. Despite their suffering, people continue to blaspheme God and refuse to repent, demonstrating their rebellion and hardness of heart.

The Sixth Bowl: The Euphrates Dried Up

Revelation 16:12-16 describes the pouring out of the sixth bowl:

> "Then the sixth angel poured out his bowl on the great river Euphrates, and its water was dried up, so that the way of the kings from the east might be prepared. And I saw three unclean spirits like frogs coming out of the mouth of the dragon, out of the mouth of the beast, and out of the mouth of the false prophet. For they are spirits of demons, performing signs, which go out to the kings of the earth and of the whole world, to gather them to the battle of that great day of God Almighty. 'Behold, I am coming as a thief. Blessed

is he who watches, and keeps his garments, lest he walk naked and they see his shame.' And they gathered them together to the place called in Hebrew, Armageddon."

- Euphrates (Εὐφράτης - Strong's G2166): Represents a significant river often associated with boundary and judgment.

- Unclean Spirits (ἀκάθαρτος πνεῦμα - Strong's G169, G4151): Symbolize demonic influences.

- Armageddon (Ἁρμαγεδών - Strong's G717): Represents the prophesied location of the final battle.

The sixth bowl dries up the Euphrates River, preparing the way for the kings of the east and gathering the forces of evil for the final battle at Armageddon. This judgment highlights the spiritual and physical preparation for the ultimate confrontation between good and evil.

The Seventh Bowl: The Earth Shaken

Revelation 16:17-21 describes the pouring out of the seventh bowl:

> "Then the seventh angel poured out his bowl into the air, and a loud voice came out of the temple of heaven, from the throne, saying, 'It is done!' And there were noises and thunderings and lightnings; and there was a great earthquake, such a mighty and great earthquake as had not occurred since men were on the earth. Now the great city was

divided into three parts, and the cities of the nations fell. And great Babylon was remembered before God, to give her the cup of the wine of the fierceness of His wrath. Then every island fled away, and the mountains were not found. And great hail from heaven fell upon men, each hailstone about the weight of a talent. Men blasphemed God because of the plague of the hail, since that plague was exceedingly great."

- Air (ἀήρ - Strong's G109): Represents the atmosphere and spiritual realm.

- It Is Done (γέγονα - Strong's G1096): Indicates the completion of God's judgments.

- Earthquake (σεισμός - Strong's G4578): Represents a significant seismic event.

- Great Babylon (Βαβυλὼν μεγάλη - Strong's G897, G3173): Symbolizes the center of worldly power and rebellion against God.

- Hailstone (χάλαζα - Strong's G5464): Represents a destructive force from heaven.

The seventh bowl brings a final, cataclysmic series of events, including a massive earthquake, the fall of cities, the destruction of Babylon, and a devastating hailstorm. This judgment signifies the culmination of God's wrath and the purification of creation.

Expository Insights

Examining the text through exhaustive Strong's Concordance reveals deeper meanings and connections:

- ἑπτα□ α□γγελος (Strong's G2033, G32): Represents the messengers of the final judgments.

- ἑπτα□ ἐσχάτος πληγή (Strong's G2033, G2078, G4127): Indicates the completion of God's wrath.

- ὀργή (Strong's G3709): Represents divine judgment and anger.

- θα□λασσα ὑάλινος (Strong's G2281, G5193): Symbolizes purity and peace mixed with judgment.

- ᾠδή Μωϋσῆς και□ ὁ ἀρνίον (Strong's G5603, G3475, G2532, G721): Represents the praise of God's deliverance and redemption.

- ναο□ς (Strong's G3485): Represents the divine sanctuary.

- καπνο□ς (Strong's G2586): Symbolizes the presence and glory of God.

- με□γας φωνη□ (Strong's G3173, G5456): Represents a commanding and authoritative voice from the temple.

- φια□λη (Strong's G5357): Represents a vessel of divine judgment.

- ὀργή Θεός (Strong's G3709, G2316): Indicates divine anger and judgment.

- κακο□ς και□ πονηρο□ς ε□λκος (Strong's G2556, G4190, G1668): Represents painful and grievous afflictions.

- χα□ραγμα θηρι□ον (Strong's G5480, G2342): Symbolizes allegiance to the Antichrist.

- θα□λασσα (Strong's G2281): Represents the world's oceans and large bodies of water.

- αἷμα (Strong's G129): Indicates widespread death and destruction.

- ψυχη□ ζῶον (Strong's G5590, G2226): Represents marine life.

- ποταμο□ς και□ πηγή (Strong's G4215, G4077): Represents fresh water sources.

- αἷμα (Strong's G129): Indicates widespread death and destruction.

- δι□καιος (Strong's G1342): Emphasizes God's justice and fairness.

- η□λιος (Strong's G2246): Represents the primary source of light and heat.

- καυματι□ζω (Strong's G2739): Indicates severe burning and suffering.

- βλασφημε□ω (Strong's G987): Represents speaking irreverently or contemptuously about God.

- θρο□νος θηρι□ον (Strong's G2362, G2342): Represents the seat of the Antichrist's power.

- σκοτο□ς (Strong's G4655): Symbolizes the absence of light and understanding.

- πο□νος (Strong's G4192): Indicates severe suffering and distress.

- Εὐφράτης (Strong's G2166): Represents a significant river often associated with boundary and judgment.

- ἀκάθαρτος πνεῦμα (Strong's G169, G4151): Symbolizes demonic influences.

- Ἁρμαγεδών (Strong's G717): Represents the prophesied location of the final battle.

- ἀήρ (Strong's G109): Represents the atmosphere and spiritual realm.

- γε□γονα (Strong's G1096): Indicates the completion of God's judgments.

- σεισμο□ς (Strong's G4578): Represents a significant seismic event.

- Βαβυλω□ν μεγα□λη (Strong's G897, G3173): Symbolizes the center of worldly power and rebellion against God.

- χα□λαζα (Strong's G5464): Represents a destructive force from heaven.

Practical Application

The vision of the seven bowls of wrath in Revelation 15-16 holds timeless relevance for believers today. Key lessons include:

1. Recognizing Jesus' Righteous Judgment: The pouring out of the bowls emphasizes Jesus' righteous anger against sin and His authority to judge. Believers are called to acknowledge and respect His justice.

2. Understanding the Consequences of Rebellion: The judgments highlight the severe consequences of rebelling against God. Believers are reminded of the seriousness of sin and the necessity of repentance.

3. Enduring Tribulation with Faith: The sufferings described in the bowl judgments call believers to remain steadfast in faith, trusting in God's ultimate deliverance and justice.

4. Anticipating the Final Purification: The judgments signify the purification of creation, preparing the way for the establishment of God's eternal kingdom. Believers can look forward to the ultimate restoration and renewal of all things.

5. Worshiping God's Righteousness: The heavenly praise in response to God's judgments encourages believers to worship and give thanks for His righteous ways and just judgments.

Conclusion

The vision of the seven bowls of wrath in Revelation 15-16 provides a profound depiction of Jesus' righteous judgment and the final purification of creation. Through the imagery of painful sores, the turning of waters to blood, scorching heat, darkness, and catastrophic events, believers are called to recognize Jesus' authority, understand the consequences of rebellion, endure tribulation with faith, anticipate the final purification, and worship God's righteousness. By examining these verses through an expository study with exhaustive Strong's Concordance, we uncover the depth of this vision and its enduring relevance for the church today. As we embrace the truths revealed in the pouring out of the seven bowls, we will be drawn into deeper worship and greater readiness for the establishment of God's eternal kingdom.

CHAPTER 09

THE WOMAN AND THE DRAGON

Revelation 12 presents a dramatic and symbolic portrayal of a cosmic battle between a woman and a dragon. The woman represents God's people, while the dragon symbolizes Satan. This chapter highlights Jesus' ultimate victory over the dragon and His protection of His followers. By examining these verses through an expository study with exhaustive Strong's Concordance, we can uncover the deeper meanings and significant truths revealed in this vision.

The Woman Clothed with the Sun

Revelation 12:1-2 introduces the woman:

> "Now a great sign appeared in heaven: a woman clothed with the sun, with the moon under her feet, and on her head a garland of twelve stars. Then being with child, she cried out in labor and in pain to give birth."

- Great Sign (σημεῖον μέγας - Strong's G4592, G3173): Indicates a significant and symbolic vision.

- Woman (γυνη□ - Strong's G1135): Represents God's people, often interpreted as Israel or the Church.

- Clothed with the Sun (περιβεβλημε□νη η□λιος - Strong's G4016, G2246): Symbolizes glory, righteousness, and divine favor.

- Moon Under Her Feet (σελη□νη υποκάτω ο΄ πούς - Strong's G4582, G5270, G4228): Represents dominion and authority.

- Garland of Twelve Stars (στε□ φανος δώδεκα αστήρ - Strong's G4735, G1427, G792): Represents the twelve tribes of Israel or the twelve apostles.

- Labor and Pain (ωδίνω και□ βασανίζω - Strong's G5605, G928): Symbolizes the struggle and anticipation of bringing forth God's purposes.

The woman clothed with the sun, standing on the moon, and crowned with twelve stars represents God's people in their glory and divine favor. Her labor and pain symbolize the struggle and anticipation of bringing forth the Messiah.

The Great Red Dragon

Revelation 12:3-4 introduces the dragon:

> "And another sign appeared in heaven: behold, a great, fiery red dragon having seven heads and ten horns, and seven diadems on his heads. His tail drew a third of the stars of heaven and threw them to the earth. And the dragon stood before the woman who was ready to give birth, to devour her Child as soon as it was born."

- Great Red Dragon (δρα□κων μεγάς πυρρὸς - Strong's G1404, G3173, G4450): Symbolizes Satan, representing evil and destruction.

- Seven Heads and Ten Horns (ἑπτα□ κεφαλή και□ δέκα κέρας - Strong's G2033, G2776, G1176, G2768): Represents authority and power.

- Seven Diadems (ἑπτα□ διάδημα - Strong's G2033, G1238): Symbolizes rulership and authority.

- Tail Drew a Third of the Stars (ουρα□ ς συρώ τρίτος ἀστήρ - Strong's G3769, G4951, G5154, G792): Represents the fall of a portion of the angels, signifying Satan's influence.

The great red dragon, with its seven heads, ten horns, and seven diadems, symbolizes Satan's power and authority. His tail sweeping a third of the stars from heaven represents the fallen angels who followed him in rebellion. The dragon's intention to devour the woman's child highlights Satan's opposition to God's redemptive plan.

The Male Child and the Woman's Escape

Revelation 12:5-6 describes the birth of the male child and the woman's escape:

> "She bore a male Child who was to rule all nations with a rod of iron. And her Child was caught up to God and His throne. Then the woman fled into the wilderness, where

she has a place prepared by God, that they should feed her there one thousand two hundred and sixty days."

- Male Child (τε□κνον α□ρσην - Strong's G5043, G730): Represents Jesus Christ, the Messiah.

- Rule All Nations (ποιμαι□νω πάς ε□θνος - Strong's G4165, G3956, G1484): Indicates Jesus' authority over all nations.

- Rod of Iron (ῥάβδος σιδηροῦς - Strong's G4464, G4603): Symbolizes strong and just rule.

- Caught Up (άρπάζω - Strong's G726): Represents Jesus' ascension to heaven.

- Wilderness (ε□ρημος - Strong's G2048): Symbolizes a place of refuge and protection.

- One Thousand Two Hundred and Sixty Days (χι□λιοι διακόσιοι εξήκοντα ήμέρα - Strong's G5507, G1250, G1835, G2250): Represents a period of divine protection and sustenance.

The male child, representing Jesus, is born to rule all nations with a rod of iron and is caught up to God's throne, symbolizing His ascension and exaltation. The woman's escape to the wilderness, where she is protected and nourished for 1,260 days, signifies God's provision and protection for His people during times of persecution.

The War in Heaven

Revelation 12:7-9 describes the war in heaven:

> "And war broke out in heaven: Michael and his angels fought with the dragon; and the dragon and his angels fought, but they did not prevail, nor was a place found for them in heaven any longer. So the great dragon was cast out, that serpent of old, called the Devil and Satan, who deceives the whole world; he was cast to the earth, and his angels were cast out with him."

- War (πο□λεμος - Strong's G4171): Represents a spiritual conflict.

- Michael (Μιχαη□λ - Strong's G3413): Represents the archangel who leads God's angelic army.

- Cast Out (βα□λλω - Strong's G906): Indicates the expulsion of Satan and his angels from heaven.

- Devil and Satan (δια□βολος και□ Σατανᾶς - Strong's G1228, G4567): Represents the accuser and adversary of God's people.

- Deceives the Whole World (πλανα□ω ο□λος οἰκουμένη - Strong's G4105, G3650, G3625): Indicates Satan's global influence and deception.

The war in heaven, led by Michael and his angels against the dragon and his angels, results in the dragon's defeat and expulsion from heaven. This cosmic battle signifies the ultimate triumph of God's forces over evil, with Satan being cast down to the earth, unable to accuse God's people before His throne any longer.

The Dragon's Persecution of the Woman

Revelation 12:10-12 describes the response to the dragon's expulsion:

> "Then I heard a loud voice saying in heaven, 'Now salvation, and strength, and the kingdom of our God, and the power of His Christ have come, for the accuser of our brethren, who accused them before our God day and night, has been cast down. And they overcame him by the blood of the Lamb and by the word of their testimony, and they did not love their lives to the death. Therefore rejoice, O heavens, and you who dwell in them! Woe to the inhabitants of the earth and the sea! For the devil has come down to you, having great wrath, because he knows that he has a short time.'"

- Salvation and Strength (σωτηρι□α και□ δύναμις - Strong's G4991, G1411): Represents the victory and power of God's kingdom.

- Accuser of Our Brethren (κατη□γωρ ἀδελφός - Strong's G2725, G80): Refers to Satan's role as the accuser.

- Blood of the Lamb (αἷμα ὁ ἀρνίον - Strong's G129, G721): Represents Jesus' sacrificial death.

- Word of Their Testimony (λο□γος μαρτυρι□α - Strong's G3056, G3141): Indicates the faithful witness of believers.

- Did Not Love Their Lives to the Death (ουκ αγαπάω ψυχή α□ χρι θάνατος - Strong's G3756, G25, G5590, G891, G2288): Represents the believers' willingness to face martyrdom for their faith.

- Great Wrath (με□ γας θυμο□ ς - Strong's G3173, G2372): Indicates Satan's intense anger and desperation.

The loud voice in heaven declares the victory of God's kingdom and the power of His Christ, emphasizing the believers' triumph over Satan through the blood of the Lamb and their testimony. While heaven rejoices, the earth faces woe due to the devil's great wrath, as he knows his time is short.

The Woman's Protection

Revelation 12:13-17 describes the dragon's persecution of the woman and her protection:

> "Now when the dragon saw that he had been cast to the earth, he persecuted the woman who gave birth to the male Child. But the woman was given two wings of a great eagle, that she might fly into the wilderness to her place, where she is nourished for a time and times and half a time, from the presence of the serpent. So the serpent spewed water out

of his mouth like a flood after the woman, that he might cause her to be carried away by the flood. But the earth helped the woman, and the earth opened its mouth and swallowed up the flood which the dragon had spewed out of his mouth. And the dragon was enraged with the woman, and he went to make war with the rest of her offspring, who keep the commandments of God and have the testimony of Jesus Christ."

- Two Wings of a Great Eagle (δυ o πτερύγιον μέγας ἀετός - Strong's G1417, G4420, G3173, G105): Symbolize divine assistance and protection.

- Wilderness (ε ρημος - Strong's G2048): Represents a place of refuge and protection.

- Time and Times and Half a Time (καιρο ς και καιρός και ἡμισής καιρός - Strong's G2540, G2540, G2532, G2255): Indicates a period of 3.5 years, symbolizing divine protection.

- Serpent (o φις - Strong's G3789): Another representation of Satan.

- Flood (ποταμο ς - Strong's G4215): Symbolizes overwhelming persecution.

- Earth Helped the Woman (γῆ βοηθε ω γυνη - Strong's G1093, G997, G1135): Represents divine intervention through natural means.

The dragon's persecution of the woman represents Satan's continued opposition to God's people. The woman is given divine protection, symbolized by the two wings of a great eagle, allowing her to escape to the wilderness where she is nourished for a time, times, and half a time. Despite the dragon's attempts to destroy her with a flood, the earth intervenes, swallowing the flood and protecting the woman. Enraged, the dragon turns his attention to making war with the rest of her offspring, who keep God's commandments and have the testimony of Jesus Christ.

Expository Insights

Examining the text through exhaustive Strong's Concordance reveals deeper meanings and connections:

- σημεῖον μέγας (Strong's G4592, G3173): Indicates a significant and symbolic vision.

- γυνη□ (Strong's G1135): Represents God's people, often interpreted as Israel or the Church.

- περιβεβλημε□νη η□λιος (Strong's G4016, G2246): Symbolizes glory, righteousness, and divine favor.

- σελη□νη ὑποκάτω ὁ πούς (Strong's G4582, G5270, G4228): Represents dominion and authority.

- στε□φανος δώδεκα ἀστήρ (Strong's G4735, G1427, G792): Represents the twelve tribes of Israel or the twelve apostles.

- ὠδίνω και□ βασανίζω (Strong's G5605, G928): Symbolizes the struggle and anticipation of bringing forth God's purposes.

- δρα□κων μεγάς πυρρός (Strong's G1404, G3173, G4450): Symbolizes Satan, representing evil and destruction.

- ἑπτα□ κεφαλή και□ δέκα κέρας (Strong's G2033, G2776, G1176, G2768): Represents authority and power.

- ἑπτα□ διάδημα (Strong's G2033, G1238): Symbolizes rulership and authority.

- ουρα□ς συρώ τρίτος ἀστήρ (Strong's G3769, G4951, G5154, G792): Represents the fall of a portion of the angels, signifying Satan's influence.

- τε□κνον α□ρσην (Strong's G5043, G730): Represents Jesus Christ, the Messiah.

- ποιμαι□νω πάς ε□θνος (Strong's G4165, G3956, G1484): Indicates Jesus' authority over all nations.

- ῥάβδος σιδηρούς (Strong's G4464, G4603): Symbolizes strong and just rule.

- ἁρπάζω (Strong's G726): Represents Jesus' ascension to heaven.

- ε□ρημος (Strong's G2048): Symbolizes a place of refuge and protection.

- χι□λιοι διακόσιοι εξήκοντα ήμέρα (Strong's G5507, G1250, G1835, G2250): Represents a period of divine protection and sustenance.

- πο□λεμος (Strong's G4171): Represents a spiritual conflict.

- Μιχαη□λ (Strong's G3413): Represents the archangel who leads God's angelic army.

- βα□λλω (Strong's G906): Indicates the expulsion of Satan and his angels from heaven.

- δια□βολος και□ Σατανᾶς (Strong's G1228, G4567): Represents the accuser and adversary of God's people.

- πλανα□ω ο□λος οἰκουμένη (Strong's G4105, G3650, G3625): Indicates Satan's global influence and deception.

- σωτηρι□α και□ δύναμις (Strong's G4991, G1411): Represents the victory and power of God's kingdom.

- κατη□γωρ ἀδελφός (Strong's G2725, G80): Refers to Satan's role as the accuser.

- αἷμα ὁ ἀρνίον (Strong's G129, G721): Represents Jesus' sacrificial death.

- λο□γος μαρτυρι□α (Strong's G3056, G3141): Indicates the faithful witness of believers.

- οὐκ ἀγαπάω ψυχή α□χρι θάνατος (Strong's G3756, G25, G5590, G891, G2288): Represents the believers' willingness to face martyrdom for their faith.

- με□γας θυμο□ς (Strong's G3173, G2372): Indicates Satan's intense anger and desperation.

- δυ□ο πτερύγιον μέγας ἀετός (Strong's G1417, G4420, G3173, G105): Symbolize divine assistance and protection.

- ε□ρημος (Strong's G2048): Represents a place of refuge and protection.

- καιρο□ς και□ καιρός και□ ἡμισής καιρός (Strong's G2540, G2540, G2532, G2255): Indicates a period of 3.5 years, symbolizing divine protection.

- ο□φις (Strong's G3789): Another representation of Satan.

- ποταμο□ς (Strong's G4215): Symbolizes overwhelming persecution.

- γῆ βοηθε□ω γυνη□ (Strong's G1093, G997, G1135): Represents divine intervention through natural means.

Practical Application

The vision of the woman and the dragon in Revelation 12 holds timeless relevance for believers today. Key lessons include:

1. Recognizing Jesus' Victory: The ultimate triumph of the male child, representing Jesus, over the dragon emphasizes Jesus' victory over Satan and evil. Believers are called to trust in Jesus' power and authority.

2. Understanding the Reality of Spiritual Warfare: The cosmic battle between the dragon and the forces of heaven highlights the ongoing spiritual conflict. Believers are reminded of the reality of spiritual warfare and the need for vigilance and reliance on God's strength.

3. Enduring Persecution with Faith: The woman's protection in the wilderness and the believers' triumph through the blood of the Lamb and their testimony call believers to endure persecution with faith, knowing that God provides refuge and victory.

4. Anticipating Divine Intervention: The divine protection and assistance given to the woman symbolize God's intervention on behalf of His people. Believers can find assurance in God's provision and care during times of trial.

5. Living as Faithful Witnesses: The believers' victory through their testimony and willingness to face martyrdom encourages believers to live as faithful witnesses, holding fast to God's commandments and the testimony of Jesus.

Conclusion

The vision of the woman and the dragon in Revelation 12 provides a profound depiction of the cosmic battle between good and evil, highlighting Jesus' victory over Satan and His protection of His followers. Through the imagery of the woman clothed with the sun, the great red dragon, the male child's triumph, and the woman's protection, believers are called to recognize Jesus' authority, understand the reality of spiritual warfare, endure persecution with faith, anticipate divine intervention, and live as faithful witnesses. By examining these verses through an expository study with exhaustive Strong's Concordance, we uncover the depth of this vision and its enduring relevance for the church today. As we embrace the truths revealed in the cosmic battle, we will be drawn into deeper trust in Jesus' victory and greater readiness to stand firm in our faith.

CHAPTER 10

THE BEATS AND THE FALSE PROPHET

Revelation 13 introduces two beasts and the false prophet, figures who deceive and persecute the faithful. Despite their temporary power, Jesus' eventual defeat of these forces illustrates His supremacy over all falsehood and oppression. By examining these verses through an expository study with exhaustive Strong's Concordance, we can uncover the deeper meanings and significant truths revealed in this vision.

The Beast from the Sea

Revelation 13:1-10 describes the first beast, which rises from the sea:

> "Then I stood on the sand of the sea. And I saw a beast rising up out of the sea, having seven heads and ten horns, and on his horns ten crowns, and on his heads a

blasphemous name. Now the beast which I saw was like a leopard, his feet were like the feet of a bear, and his mouth like the mouth of a lion. The dragon gave him his power, his throne, and great authority. And I saw one of his heads as if it had been mortally wounded, and his deadly wound was healed. And all the world marveled and followed the beast. So they worshiped the dragon who gave authority to the beast; and they worshiped the beast, saying, 'Who is like the beast? Who is able to make war with him?' And he was given a mouth speaking great things and blasphemies, and he was given authority to continue for forty-two months. Then he opened his mouth in blasphemy against God, to blaspheme His name, His tabernacle, and those who dwell in heaven. And it was granted to him to make war with the saints and to overcome them. And authority was given him over every tribe, tongue, and nation. All who dwell on the earth will worship him, whose names have not been written in the Book of Life of the Lamb slain from the foundation of the world. If anyone has an ear, let him hear. He who leads into captivity shall go into captivity; he who kills with the sword must be killed with the sword. Here is the patience and the faith of the saints."

- Beast (θηρι□ον - Strong's G2342): Represents a powerful, oppressive empire or ruler.

- Sea (θα□λασσα - Strong's G2281): Symbolizes chaos and the nations.

- Seven Heads and Ten Horns (έπτα□ κεφαλή και□ δέκα κέρας - Strong's G2033, G2776, G1176, G2768): Represents authority and power.

- Blasphemous Name (βλασφημι□α ο□νομα - Strong's G988, G3686): Indicates defiance against God.

- Leopard, Bear, Lion (πα□ρδαλις, α□ρκος, λέων - Strong's G3917, G715, G3023): Symbolizes swiftness, strength, and ferocity.

- Dragon (δρα□κων - Strong's G1404): Represents Satan.

- Power, Throne, Authority (δυ□ναμις, θρόνος, έξουσία - Strong's G1411, G2362, G1849): Indicates Satan's delegation of power.

- Mortally Wounded, Healed (σφα□ζω, θεραπευ□ω - Strong's G4969, G2323): Suggests a counterfeit resurrection.

- Forty-Two Months (τεσσερα□κοντα δυ□ο μη□ν - Strong's G5062, G1417, G3376): Represents a limited period of authority.

- Blaspheme (βλασφημε□ω - Strong's G987): Represents speaking against God.

- Book of Life (βι□βλος ζωη□ - Strong's G976, G2222): Symbolizes eternal life in Christ.

- Patience and Faith (ὑπομονή καὶ πίστις - Strong's G5281, G2532, G4102): Indicates endurance and trust in God.

The beast from the sea, with its composite features of a leopard, bear, and lion, symbolizes a powerful and oppressive empire or ruler. Empowered by the dragon (Satan), this beast blasphemes God and persecutes the saints for forty-two months. Despite its apparent authority and power, the beast's reign is limited, and its blasphemies and oppression are ultimately futile.

The Beast from the Earth

Revelation 13:11-18 describes the second beast, which rises from the earth:

> "Then I saw another beast coming up out of the earth, and he had two horns like a lamb and spoke like a dragon. And he exercises all the authority of the first beast in his presence, and causes the earth and those who dwell in it to worship the first beast, whose deadly wound was healed. He performs great signs, so that he even makes fire come down from heaven on the earth in the sight of men. And he deceives those who dwell on the earth by those signs which he was granted to do in the sight of the beast, telling those who dwell on the earth to make an image to the beast who was wounded by the sword and lived. He was granted power

to give breath to the image of the beast, that the image of the beast should both speak and cause as many as would not worship the image of the beast to be killed. He causes all, both small and great, rich and poor, free and slave, to receive a mark on their right hand or on their foreheads, and that no one may buy or sell except one who has the mark or the name of the beast, or the number of his name. Here is wisdom. Let him who has understanding calculate the number of the beast, for it is the number of a man: His number is 666."

- Beast (θηρι□ον - Strong's G2342): Represents a powerful, deceptive religious or political leader.

- Earth (γῆ - Strong's G1093): Symbolizes stability and the realm of human activity.

- Two Horns Like a Lamb (δυ□ο κέρας ὡς ἀρνίον - Strong's G1417, G2768, G5613, G721): Indicates a deceptive appearance of gentleness.

- Spoke Like a Dragon (λαλε□ω ὡς δράκων - Strong's G2980, G5613, G1404): Reveals its true, satanic nature.

- Great Signs (με□γας σημεῖον - Strong's G3173, G4592): Represents deceptive miracles.

- Fire from Heaven (πῦρ ἐκ οὐρανός - Strong's G4442, G1537, G3772): Symbolizes a counterfeit display of divine power.

- Deceives (πλανα□ω - Strong's G4105): Indicates leading people astray.

- Image of the Beast (εἰκών θηρίον - Strong's G1504, G2342): Represents idolatrous worship.

- Breath to the Image (πνεῦμα εἰκών - Strong's G4151, G1504): Suggests a false semblance of life.

- Mark (χα□ραγμα - Strong's G5480): Symbolizes allegiance and control.

- Number of the Beast (ἀριθμός θηρίον - Strong's G706, G2342): Represents the identification of the beast.

- 666 (εξακόσιοι εξάκοντα ε□ξ - Strong's G5516): Indicates the number of a man, symbolizing imperfection and evil.

The beast from the earth, with its lamb-like appearance and dragon-like speech, symbolizes a powerful and deceptive religious or political leader. This beast performs great signs and deceives the world, leading people to worship the first beast and receive its mark. The mark, representing allegiance and control, is necessary for economic transactions, indicating the beast's totalitarian control over society.

The False Prophet

Revelation 13:11-18 introduces the false prophet, who promotes the worship of the first beast and performs deceptive signs. The false prophet, with its deceptive appearance and miraculous signs, leads the world astray and enforces the worship of the first beast. The false prophet's actions underscore the theme of deception and falsehood, highlighting the contrast between the true Christ and the counterfeit powers.

Expository Insights

Examining the text through exhaustive Strong's Concordance reveals deeper meanings and connections:

- θηρι□ον (Strong's G2342): Represents a powerful, oppressive empire or ruler.

- θα□λασσα (Strong's G2281): Symbolizes chaos and the nations.

- ἑπτα□ κεφαλή και□ δέκα κέρας (Strong's G2033, G2776, G1176, G2768): Represents authority and power.

- βλασφημι□α ο□νομα (Strong's G988, G3686): Indicates defiance against God.

- πα□ρδαλις, α□ρκος, λέων (Strong's G3917, G715, G3023): Symbolizes swiftness, strength, and ferocity.

- δρα□κων (Strong's G1404): Represents Satan.

- δυ□ναμις, θρόνος, ἐξουσία (Strong's G1411, G2362, G1849): Indicates Satan's delegation of power.

- σφα□ζω, θεραπευ□ω (Strong's G4969, G2323): Suggests a counterfeit resurrection.

- τεσσερα□κοντα δυ□ο μη□ν (Strong's G5062, G1417, G3376): Represents a limited period of authority.

- βλασφημε□ω (Strong's G987): Represents speaking against God.

- βι□βλος ζωη□ (Strong's G976, G2222): Symbolizes eternal life in Christ.

- ὑπομονή και□ πίστις (Strong's G5281, G2532, G4102): Indicates endurance and trust in God.

- γῆ (Strong's G1093): Symbolizes stability and the realm of human activity.

- δυ□ο κέρας ὡς ἀρνίον (Strong's G1417, G2768, G5613, G721): Indicates a deceptive appearance of gentleness.

- λαλε□ω ὡς δράκων (Strong's G2980, G5613, G1404): Reveals its true, satanic nature.

- με□γας σημεῖον (Strong's G3173, G4592): Represents deceptive miracles.

- πῦρ ἐκ οὐρανός (Strong's G4442, G1537, G3772): Symbolizes a counterfeit display of divine power.

- πλανα□ω (Strong's G4105): Indicates leading people astray.

- εἰκών θηρίον (Strong's G1504, G2342): Represents idolatrous worship.

- πνεῦμα εἰκών (Strong's G4151, G1504): Suggests a false semblance of life.

- χα☐ραγμα (Strong's G5480): Symbolizes allegiance and control.

- ἀριθμός θηρίον (Strong's G706, G2342): Represents the identification of the beast.

- εξακόσιοι εξάκοντα ε☐ ξ (Strong's G5516): Indicates the number of a man, symbolizing imperfection and evil.

Practical Application

The vision of the beasts and the false prophet in Revelation 13 holds timeless relevance for believers today. Key lessons include:

1. Recognizing Deception: The deceptive nature of the beasts and the false prophet highlights the importance of discernment. Believers are called to be vigilant and grounded in the truth to recognize and resist falsehood.

2. Understanding the Reality of Spiritual Warfare: The vision underscores the ongoing spiritual conflict and the forces of evil that seek to deceive and oppress. Believers are reminded of the reality of spiritual warfare and the need for spiritual armor (Ephesians 6:10-18).

3. Enduring Persecution with Faith: The persecution and oppression by the beasts call believers to remain steadfast

in faith, knowing that Jesus ultimately triumphs over all forces of evil.

4. Trusting in Jesus' Supremacy: Despite the temporary power of the beasts and the false prophet, Jesus' eventual defeat of these forces illustrates His supremacy. Believers are encouraged to trust in Jesus' ultimate victory and His authority over all creation.

5. Living as Faithful Witnesses: The emphasis on the saints' endurance and faith highlights the call to live as faithful witnesses, holding fast to God's commandments and the testimony of Jesus.

Conclusion

The vision of the beasts and the false prophet in Revelation 13 provides a profound depiction of the forces of deception and oppression that oppose God's people. Through the imagery of the beast from the sea, the beast from the earth, and the false prophet, believers are called to recognize deception, understand the reality of spiritual warfare, endure persecution with faith, trust in Jesus' supremacy, and live as faithful witnesses. By examining these verses through an expository study with exhaustive Strong's Concordance, we uncover the depth of this vision and its enduring relevance for the church today. As we embrace the truths revealed in the portrayal of the beasts and the false prophet, we will be drawn into deeper trust in Jesus' victory and greater readiness to stand firm in our faith.

CHAPTER 11

THE FALL OF BABYLON

Revelation 17-18 vividly portrays the fall of Babylon, symbolizing the corrupt systems and powers of the world that stand in opposition to God. Jesus' judgment against Babylon signifies the end of evil's reign and the establishment of His just and holy kingdom. By examining these chapters through an expository study with exhaustive Strong's Concordance, we can uncover the deeper meanings and significant truths revealed in this vision.

The Great Prostitute and the Beast

Revelation 17:1-6 introduces the vision of the great prostitute and the beast:

> "Then one of the seven angels who had the seven bowls came and talked with me, saying to me, 'Come, I will show you the judgment of the great harlot who sits on many waters, with whom the kings of the earth committed fornication, and the inhabitants of the earth were made drunk with the wine of her fornication.' So he carried me away in the Spirit into the wilderness. And I saw a woman sitting on a scarlet beast which was full of names of blasphemy, having seven heads and ten horns. The woman was arrayed in purple and scarlet, and adorned with gold and precious stones and pearls, having in her hand a golden cup full of abominations and the filthiness of her fornication. And on her forehead a name was written: MYSTERY, BABYLON THE GREAT, THE MOTHER OF HARLOTS AND OF THE ABOMINATIONS OF THE EARTH. I saw the woman, drunk with the blood of the saints and with the blood of the martyrs of Jesus. And when I saw her, I marveled with great amazement."

- Great Harlot (πο□ρνη μεγα□λη - Strong's G4204, G3173): Symbolizes the corrupt and idolatrous systems of the world.

- Many Waters (πολυ□ς υ□δωρ - Strong's G4183, G5204): Represents peoples, multitudes, nations, and tongues (Revelation 17:15).

- Fornication (πορνει□α - Strong's G4202): Symbolizes idolatry and unfaithfulness to God.

- Scarlet Beast (θηρι□ον κο□κκινος - Strong's G2342, G2847): Represents a powerful and blasphemous political power.

- Seven Heads and Ten Horns (έπτα□ κεφαλή και□ δέκα κέρας - Strong's G2033, G2776, G1176, G2768): Represents authority and power (Revelation 17:9-12).

- Purple and Scarlet (πορφυ□ρα και□ κόκκινος - Strong's G4209, G2847): Symbolizes wealth and royalty.

- Golden Cup (χρυσοῦς ποτήριον - Strong's G5552, G4221): Represents external allure and internal corruption.

- Abominations (βδε□λυγμα - Strong's G946): Indicates detestable practices and idolatry.

- Drunk with Blood (μεθυ□ω αἷμα - Strong's G3184, G129): Represents persecution and martyrdom of the saints.

The great prostitute, adorned in purple and scarlet and sitting on a scarlet beast, symbolizes the corrupt and idolatrous systems of the world. Her intoxication with the blood of the saints highlights her role in persecuting God's people. The scarlet beast represents a powerful political entity that supports her.

The Mystery of the Woman and the Beast

Revelation 17:7-18 explains the mystery of the woman and the beast:

> "But the angel said to me, 'Why did you marvel? I will tell you the mystery of the woman and of the beast that carries her, which has the seven heads and the ten horns. The beast that you saw was, and is not, and will ascend out of the bottomless pit and go to perdition. And those who dwell on the earth will marvel, whose names are not written in the Book of Life from the foundation of the world, when they see the beast that was, and is not, and yet is. Here is the mind which has wisdom: The seven heads are seven mountains on which the woman sits. There are also seven kings. Five have fallen, one is, and the other has not yet come. And when he comes, he must continue a short time. The beast that was, and is not, is himself also the eighth, and is of the seven, and is going to perdition. The ten horns which you saw are ten kings who have received no kingdom as yet, but they receive authority for one hour as kings with the beast. These are of one mind, and they will give their power and authority to the beast. These will make war with the Lamb, and the Lamb will overcome them, for He is Lord of lords and King of kings; and those who are with Him are called, chosen, and faithful.' Then he said to me, 'The waters which you saw, where the harlot sits, are peoples, multitudes, nations, and tongues. And

the ten horns which you saw on the beast, these will hate the harlot, make her desolate and naked, eat her flesh and burn her with fire. For God has put it into their hearts to fulfill His purpose, to be of one mind, and to give their kingdom to the beast, until the words of God are fulfilled. And the woman whom you saw is that great city which reigns over the kings of the earth.'"

- Mystery (μυστη□ριον - Strong's G3466): Indicates a revealed secret or divine truth.

- Bottomless Pit (α□βυσσος - Strong's G12): Represents the abyss or the realm of the dead.

- Perdition (ἀπώλεια - Strong's G684): Indicates destruction or ruin.

- Seven Mountains (ἑπτα□ ο□ρος - Strong's G2033, G3735): Represents a place of great authority, often interpreted as Rome.

- Seven Kings (ἑπτα□ βασιλεύς - Strong's G2033, G935): Represents successive rulers or empires.

- Ten Kings (δε□κα βασιλευ□ς - Strong's G1176, G935): Symbolizes a confederation of rulers.

- One Hour (μι□α ω□ρα - Strong's G1520, G5610): Indicates a brief period of authority.

- War with the Lamb (πολεμε□ω το□ ἀρνίον - Strong's G4170, G721): Represents opposition to Jesus.

- Lord of Lords and King of Kings (κυ□ριος κυρίων και□ βασιλευ□ς βασιλέων - Strong's G2962, G2962, G935, G935): Emphasizes Jesus' supreme authority.

- Desolate and Naked (ἐρημόω και□ γυμνός - Strong's G2049, G1131): Indicates complete destruction and exposure.

The angel explains the symbolism of the woman and the beast, revealing the nature of their power and influence. The seven heads represent seven mountains and seven kings, while the ten horns represent ten kings who will give their authority to the beast for a brief period. These forces will make war against the Lamb, but Jesus, the Lord of lords and King of kings, will overcome them. The woman's desolation by the ten kings signifies the internal betrayal and ultimate destruction of corrupt systems.

The Fall of Babylon the Great

Revelation 18:1-8 proclaims the fall of Babylon:

> "After these things I saw another angel coming down from heaven, having great authority, and the earth was illuminated with his glory. And he cried mightily with a loud voice, saying, 'Babylon the great is fallen, is fallen, and has become a dwelling place of demons, a prison for every foul spirit, and a cage for every unclean and hated bird! For all the nations have drunk of the wine of the wrath of her

fornication, the kings of the earth have committed fornication with her, and the merchants of the earth have become rich through the abundance of her luxury.' And I heard another voice from heaven saying, 'Come out of her, my people, lest you share in her sins, and lest you receive of her plagues. For her sins have reached to heaven, and God has remembered her iniquities. Render to her just as she rendered to you, and repay her double according to her works; in the cup which she has mixed, mix double for her. In the measure that she glorified herself and lived luxuriously, in the same measure give her torment and sorrow; for she says in her heart, "I sit as queen, and am no widow, and will not see sorrow." Therefore her plagues will come in one day—death and mourning and famine. And she will be utterly burned with fire, for strong is the Lord God who judges her.'"

- Babylon the Great (Βαβυλω□ν ή μεγάλη - Strong's G897, G3173): Symbolizes the corrupt and idolatrous systems of the world.

- Dwelling Place of Demons (κατοικητη□ριον δαιμο□νιον - Strong's G2732, G1140): Indicates a place of evil habitation.

- Foul Spirit (ἀκάθαρτος πνεῦμα - Strong's G169, G4151): Represents unclean and demonic influences.

- Unclean and Hated Bird (ἀκάθαρτος καὶ μισέω οῧρνεον - Strong's G169, G3404, G3732): Symbolizes impurity and detestable practices.

- Wine of the Wrath (οἶνος θυμός - Strong's G3631, G2372): Represents intoxicating and destructive influence.

- Come Out of Her (ἐξ ἐῧρχομαι - Strong's G1537, G2064): Calls for separation from corruption.

- Double Repayment (διπλοῧς - Strong's G1362): Indicates complete and just retribution.

The angel's proclamation of Babylon's fall emphasizes the complete and irrevocable judgment against the corrupt systems of the world. Babylon's fall is marked by desolation, demonic habitation, and divine retribution. The call to "come out of her" urges God's people to separate themselves from the corruption and impending judgment.

The Lament of the Kings, Merchants, and Mariners

Revelation 18:9-19 describes the lament of those who profited from Babylon:

> "The kings of the earth who committed fornication and lived luxuriously with her will weep and lament for her, when they see the smoke of her burning, standing at a distance for fear of her torment, saying, 'Alas, alas, that great city Babylon, that mighty city! For in one hour your judgment has come.' And the merchants of the earth will weep and mourn

over her, for no one buys their merchandise anymore: merchandise of gold and silver, precious stones and pearls, fine linen and purple, silk and scarlet, every kind of citron wood, every kind of object of ivory, every kind of object of most precious wood, bronze, iron, and marble; and cinnamon and incense, fragrant oil and frankincense, wine and oil, fine flour and wheat, cattle and sheep, horses and chariots, and bodies and souls of men. The fruit that your soul longed for has gone from you, and all the things which are rich and splendid have gone from you, and you shall find them no more at all. The merchants of these things, who became rich by her, will stand at a distance for fear of her torment, weeping and wailing, and saying, 'Alas, alas, that great city that was clothed in fine linen, purple, and scarlet, and adorned with gold and precious stones and pearls! For in one hour such great riches came to nothing.' Every shipmaster, all who travel by ship, sailors, and as many as trade on the sea, stood at a distance and cried out when they saw the smoke of her burning, saying, 'What is like this great city?' They threw dust on their heads and cried out, weeping and wailing, and saying, 'Alas, alas, that great city, in which all who had ships on the sea became rich by her wealth! For in one hour she is made desolate.'"

- Kings of the Earth (βασιλευ□ς η̒ γη̃ - Strong's G935, G1093): Represents political leaders who benefited from Babylon.

- Merchants of the Earth (ε□μπορος η̒ γη̃ - Strong's G1713, G1093): Represents those who profited from trade with Babylon.

- Weep and Lament (κλαι□ω και□ κόπτω - Strong's G2799, G2875): Indicates mourning and sorrow.

- Merchandise (γο□μος - Strong's G1117): Represents the wealth and luxury goods associated with Babylon.

- In One Hour (μι□α ω□ρα - Strong's G1520, G5610): Indicates sudden and complete judgment.

The lament of the kings, merchants, and mariners underscores the sudden and total destruction of Babylon. Those who profited from her luxury and corruption mourn her downfall, recognizing the loss of their wealth and the swiftness of her judgment.

Rejoicing in Heaven

Revelation 18:20-24 calls for rejoicing over Babylon's fall:

> "'Rejoice over her, O heaven, and you holy apostles and prophets, for God has avenged you on her!' Then a mighty angel took up a stone like a great millstone and threw it into the sea, saying, 'Thus with violence the great city

Babylon shall be thrown down, and shall not be found anymore. The sound of harpists, musicians, flutists, and trumpeters shall not be heard in you anymore. No craftsman of any craft shall be found in you anymore, and the sound of a millstone shall not be heard in you anymore. The light of a lamp shall not shine in you anymore, and the voice of bridegroom and bride shall not be heard in you anymore. For your merchants were the great men of the earth, for by your sorcery all the nations were deceived. And in her was found the blood of prophets and saints, and of all who were slain on the earth.'"

- Rejoice (χαι□ρω - Strong's G5463): Represents celebration and exultation.

- Millstone (μυ□λος - Strong's G3458): Symbolizes complete and irreversible destruction.

- Violence (βι□αιος - Strong's G973): Indicates forceful and decisive judgment.

- Sorcery (φαρμακει□α - Strong's G5331): Represents deception and manipulation.

- Blood of Prophets and Saints (αἷμα προφήτης και□ α□γιος - Strong's G129, G4396, G40): Highlights Babylon's persecution and martyrdom of God's people.

Heaven rejoices over the fall of Babylon, recognizing God's just vengeance for the blood of prophets and saints. The mighty angel's act of throwing a great millstone into the sea symbolizes Babylon's complete and irreversible destruction.

Expository Insights

Examining the text through exhaustive Strong's Concordance reveals deeper meanings and connections:

- πο□ρνη μεγα□λη (Strong's G4204, G3173): Symbolizes the corrupt and idolatrous systems of the world.

- πολυ□ς υ□δωρ (Strong's G4183, G5204): Represents peoples, multitudes, nations, and tongues.

- πορνει□α (Strong's G4202): Symbolizes idolatry and unfaithfulness to God.

- θηρι□ον κο□κκινος (Strong's G2342, G2847): Represents a powerful and blasphemous political power.

- ἑπτα□ κεφαλή και□ δέκα κέρας (Strong's G2033, G2776, G1176, G2768): Represents authority and power.

- πορφυ□ρα και□ κόκκινος (Strong's G4209, G2847): Symbolizes wealth and royalty.

- χρυσοῦς ποτήριον (Strong's G5552, G4221): Represents external allure and internal corruption.

- βδε□λυγμα (Strong's G946): Indicates detestable practices and idolatry.

- μεθυ☐ω αἷμα (Strong's G3184, G129): Represents persecution and martyrdom of the saints.

- μυστη☐ριον (Strong's G3466): Indicates a revealed secret or divine truth.

- α☐βυσσος (Strong's G12): Represents the abyss or the realm of the dead.

- ἀπώλεια (Strong's G684): Indicates destruction or ruin.

- ἑπτα☐ ο☐ρος (Strong's G2033, G3735): Represents a place of great authority, often interpreted as Rome.

- ἑπτα☐ βασιλεύς (Strong's G2033, G935): Represents successive rulers or empires.

- δε☐κα βασιλευ☐ς (Strong's G1176, G935): Symbolizes a confederation of rulers.

- μι☐α ω☐ρα (Strong's G1520, G5610): Indicates a brief period of authority.

- πολεμε☐ω το☐ ἀρνίον (Strong's G4170, G721): Represents opposition to Jesus.

- κυ☐ριος κυρίων και☐ βασιλευ☐ς βασιλέων (Strong's G2962, G2962, G935, G935): Emphasizes Jesus' supreme authority.

- ἐρημόω και☐ γυμνός (Strong's G2049, G1131): Indicates complete destruction and exposure.

- Βαβυλω□ν ἡ μεγάλη (Strong's G897, G3173): Symbolizes the corrupt and idolatrous systems of the world.

- κατοικητη□ριον δαιμο□νιον (Strong's G2732, G1140): Indicates a place of evil habitation.

- ἀκάθαρτος πνε ῦμα (Strong's G169, G4151): Represents unclean and demonic influences.

- ἀκάθαρτος και□ μισέω ο□ρνεον (Strong's G169, G3404, G3732): Symbolizes impurity and detestable practices.

- οἶνος θυμός (Strong's G3631, G2372): Represents intoxicating and destructive influence.

- ἐξ ε□ρχομαι (Strong's G1537, G2064): Calls for separation from corruption.

- διπλο□ς (Strong's G1362): Indicates complete and just retribution.

- βασιλευ□ς ἡ γῆ (Strong's G935, G1093): Represents political leaders who benefited from Babylon.

- ε□μπορος ἡ γῆ (Strong's G1713, G1093): Represents those who profited from trade with Babylon.

- κλαι□ω και□ κόπτω (Strong's G2799, G2875): Indicates mourning and sorrow.

- γο□μος (Strong's G1117): Represents the wealth and luxury goods associated with Babylon.

- μί□α ω□ρα (Strong's G1520, G5610): Indicates sudden and complete judgment.

- χαι□ρω (Strong's G5463): Represents celebration and exultation.

- μυ□λος (Strong's G3458): Symbolizes complete and irreversible destruction.

- βι□αιος (Strong's G973): Indicates forceful and decisive judgment.

- φαρμακει□α (Strong's G5331): Represents deception and manipulation.

- αἷμα προφήτης και□ α□γιος (Strong's G129, G4396, G40): Highlights Babylon's persecution and martyrdom of God's people.

Practical Application

The vision of the fall of Babylon in Revelation 17-18 holds timeless relevance for believers today. Key lessons include:

1. Recognizing the Corruption of Worldly Systems: The portrayal of Babylon as a great prostitute highlights the pervasive corruption and idolatry of worldly systems. Believers are called to recognize and reject these influences.

2. Understanding the Reality of Divine Judgment: The fall of Babylon emphasizes the certainty and severity of God's

judgment against evil. Believers are reminded of the seriousness of sin and the need for repentance.

3. Separating from Corruption: The call to "come out of her" urges believers to separate themselves from corrupt practices and systems to avoid sharing in their judgment.

4. Trusting in Jesus' Victory: Despite the temporary power of corrupt systems, Jesus' judgment against Babylon signifies His ultimate victory and the establishment of His just and holy kingdom. Believers can trust in His authority and justice.

5. Living as Faithful Witnesses: The emphasis on the blood of the prophets and saints encourages believers to live as faithful witnesses, holding fast to God's commandments and the testimony of Jesus.

Conclusion

The vision of the fall of Babylon in Revelation 17-18 provides a profound depiction of the judgment against the corrupt systems of the world and the ultimate triumph of Jesus. Through the imagery of the great prostitute, the beast, and the angelic proclamations, believers are called to recognize corruption, understand the reality of divine judgment, separate from evil, trust in Jesus' victory, and live as faithful witnesses. By examining these verses through an expository study with exhaustive Strong's Concordance, we uncover the depth of this vision and its enduring relevance for the church today. As we embrace the truths revealed in the fall of Babylon, we will be drawn into deeper trust in Jesus' justice and greater readiness to stand firm in our faith.

CHAPTER 12

THE TRIUMPH OF JESUS

Revelation 19 portrays the glorious triumph of Jesus as a victorious warrior, riding a white horse and leading the armies of heaven. His defeat of the beast and the false prophet, followed by the celebration of His reign, underscores His role as the King of Kings and Lord of Lords. By examining these verses through an expository study with exhaustive Strong's Concordance, we can uncover the deeper meanings and significant truths revealed in this vision.

The Heavenly Multitude Praises God

Revelation 19:1-6 describes the praise of the heavenly multitude:

> "After these things I heard a loud voice of a great multitude in heaven, saying, 'Alleluia! Salvation and glory and honor and power belong to the Lord our God! For true and righteous are His judgments, because He has judged the great harlot who corrupted the earth with her fornication; and He has avenged on her the blood of His servants shed by her.' Again they said, 'Alleluia! Her smoke rises up forever and ever!' And the twenty-four elders and the four living creatures fell down and worshiped God who sat on the throne, saying, 'Amen! Alleluia!' Then a voice came from the throne, saying, 'Praise our God, all you His servants and those who fear Him, both small and great!' And I heard, as it were, the voice of a great multitude, as the sound of many waters and as the sound of mighty thunderings, saying, 'Alleluia! For the Lord God Omnipotent reigns!'"

- Great Multitude (ὄχλος πολύς - Strong's G3793, G4183): Represents a vast number of people.

- Alleluia (αλληλούϊα - Strong's G239): Means "Praise the Lord."

- Salvation (σωτηρι□α - Strong's G4991): Indicates deliverance and rescue.

- Glory (δο□ξα - Strong's G1391): Represents honor and splendor.

- Honor (τιμη□ - Strong's G5092): Indicates value and esteem.

- Power (δυ□ναμις - Strong's G1411): Represents strength and ability.

- True and Righteous Judgments (αληθινός και□ δίκαιος κρίσις - Strong's G228, G1342, G2920): Emphasizes the fairness and justice of God's actions.

- Twenty-Four Elders (ει□κοσι τέσσαρες πρεσβύτερος - Strong's G1501, G5064, G4245): Symbolize the redeemed representatives of the Church.

- Four Living Creatures (τε□σσαρες ζῶον - Strong's G5064, G2226): Represent angelic beings or cherubim.

- Servants (δοῦλος - Strong's G1401): Refers to God's faithful followers.

- Many Waters (υ□δωρ πολύς - Strong's G5204, G4183): Symbolizes a powerful and overwhelming sound.

- Mighty Thunderings (βροντη□ μεγα□λη - Strong's G1027, G3173): Indicates the powerful voice of God.

The heavenly multitude's praise emphasizes the justice and righteousness of God's judgments. Their worship and the repeated "Alleluia" highlight the joy and reverence in response to God's victory over evil.

The Marriage Supper of the Lamb

Revelation 19:7-10 describes the celebration of the marriage supper of the Lamb:

> "'Let us be glad and rejoice and give Him glory, for the marriage of the Lamb has come, and His wife has made herself ready.' And to her it was granted to be arrayed in fine linen, clean and bright, for the fine linen is the righteous acts of the saints. Then he said to me, 'Write: "Blessed are those who are called to the marriage supper of the Lamb!"' And he said to me, 'These are the true sayings of God.' And I fell at his feet to worship him. But he said to me, 'See that you do not do that! I am your fellow servant, and of your brethren who have the testimony of Jesus. Worship God! For the testimony of Jesus is the spirit of prophecy.'"

- Marriage of the Lamb (γα□μος τοῦ ἀρνίου - Strong's G1062, G721): Symbolizes the union of Christ and His Church.

- Wife (γυνη□ - Strong's G1135): Represents the Church, the bride of Christ.

- Fine Linen (βυ□σσινος λαμπρο□ς καθαρο□ς - Strong's G1039, G2986, G2513): Symbolizes purity and righteousness.

- Righteous Acts (δικαι□ωμα - Strong's G1345): Represents the deeds of the saints.

- Blessed (μακα□ριος - Strong's G3107): Indicates a state of happiness and favor.

- Marriage Supper (δεῖπνον γάμος - Strong's G1173, G1062): Represents the celebratory feast of the union between Christ and His Church.

- Testimony of Jesus (μαρτυρι□α Ἰησοῦς - Strong's G3141, G2424): Refers to the witness and proclamation of Jesus.

- Spirit of Prophecy (πνεῦμα προφητεία - Strong's G4151, G4394): Indicates the Holy Spirit's role in revealing and testifying about Jesus.

The marriage supper of the Lamb symbolizes the joyous union between Christ and His Church. The fine linen represents the righteousness of the saints, and the celebration highlights the blessedness of those called to participate in this divine union.

The Rider on the White Horse

Revelation 19:11-16 describes the triumphant return of Jesus:

> "Now I saw heaven opened, and behold, a white horse. And He who sat on him was called Faithful and True, and in righteousness He judges and makes war. His eyes were

like a flame of fire, and on His head were many crowns. He had a name written that no one knew except Himself. He was clothed with a robe dipped in blood, and His name is called The Word of God. And the armies in heaven, clothed in fine linen, white and clean, followed Him on white horses. Now out of His mouth goes a sharp sword, that with it He should strike the nations. And He Himself will rule them with a rod of iron. He Himself treads the winepress of the fierceness and wrath of Almighty God. And He has on His robe and on His thigh a name written: KING OF KINGS AND LORD OF LORDS."

- White Horse (λευκο□ς □ππος - Strong's G3022, G2462): Symbolizes victory and purity.

- Faithful and True (πιστο□ς και□ αληθινός - Strong's G4103, G228): Indicates Jesus' reliability and truthfulness.

- Flame of Fire (φλο□ξ πῦρ - Strong's G5395, G4442): Represents penetrating judgment.

- Many Crowns (πολυ□ς διάδημα - Strong's G4183, G1238): Symbolizes supreme authority and kingship.

- The Word of God (λο□γος τοῦ Θεοῦ - Strong's G3056, G2316): Identifies Jesus as the divine Logos.

- Armies in Heaven (στρατευ□ματα ὁ ουρανός - Strong's G4753, G3772): Represents the heavenly hosts.

- Sharp Sword (ϱομφαι□α ὀξύς - Strong's G4501, G3691): Symbolizes the power of Jesus' word.

- Rod of Iron (ϱάβδος σιδηϱοῦς - Strong's G4464, G4603): Represents Jesus' strong and just rule.

- Winepress of Wrath (ληνο□ς ὀϱγή - Strong's G3025, G3709): Symbolizes the execution of divine judgment.

- King of Kings and Lord of Lords (βασιλευ□ς βασιλέων και□ κύϱιος κυϱίων - Strong's G935, G935, G2962, G2962): Emphasizes Jesus' supreme authority over all rulers.

The vision of Jesus riding a white horse, leading the armies of heaven, and executing judgment underscores His role as the triumphant and righteous King. His titles, Faithful and True, The Word of God, and King of Kings and Lord of Lords, highlight His divine authority and sovereignty.

The Defeat of the Beast and the False Prophet

Revelation 19:17-21 describes the defeat of the beast and the false prophet:

> "Then I saw an angel standing in the sun; and he cried with a loud voice, saying to all the birds that fly in the midst of heaven, 'Come and gather together for the supper of the great God, that you may eat the flesh of kings, the flesh of captains, the flesh of mighty men, the flesh of horses and of those who sit on them, and the flesh of all people, free and slave, both small and great.' And I saw the beast, the kings of

the earth, and their armies, gathered together to make war against Him who sat on the horse and against His army. Then the beast was captured, and with him the false prophet who worked signs in his presence, by which he deceived those who received the mark of the beast and those who worshiped his image. These two were cast alive into the lake of fire burning with brimstone. And the rest were killed with the sword which proceeded from the mouth of Him who sat on the horse. And all the birds were filled with their flesh."

- Angel (α□γγελος - Strong's G32): Represents a messenger of God.

- Supper of the Great God (δεῖπνον ὁ μεγάλος Θεός - Strong's G1173, G3173, G2316): Symbolizes the divine retribution against God's enemies.

- Beast (θηρι□ον - Strong's G2342): Represents the oppressive and blasphemous political power.

- False Prophet (ψευδοπροφη□της - Strong's G5578): Represents the deceptive religious leader.

- Lake of Fire (λι□μνη πῦρ - Strong's G3041, G4442): Symbolizes the final destination of judgment and eternal punishment.

- Sword from His Mouth (ρομφαι□α ἐκ ὁ στόμα - Strong's G4501, G1537, G3588, G4750): Represents the power of Jesus' word to execute judgment.

The defeat of the beast and the false prophet, cast into the lake of fire, and the subsequent destruction of their armies, emphasize the finality and completeness of Jesus' victory over evil. The call to the birds to feast on the flesh of the defeated symbolizes the total destruction and humiliation of God's enemies.

Expository Insights

Examining the text through exhaustive Strong's Concordance reveals deeper meanings and connections:

- οῦ χλος πολύς (Strong's G3793, G4183): Represents a vast number of people.

- αλληλούϊα (Strong's G239): Means "Praise the Lord."

- σωτηρι α (Strong's G4991): Indicates deliverance and rescue.

- δο ξα (Strong's G1391): Represents honor and splendor.

- τιμη (Strong's G5092): Indicates value and esteem.

- δυ ναμις (Strong's G1411): Represents strength and ability.

- αληθινός και δίκαιος κρίσις (Strong's G228, G1342, G2920): Emphasizes the fairness and justice of God's actions.

- ει κοσι τέσσαρες πρεσβύτερος (Strong's G1501, G5064, G4245): Symbolize the redeemed representatives of the Church.

- τε□ σσαρες ζῶον (Strong's G5064, G2226): Represent angelic beings or cherubim.

- δοῦλος (Strong's G1401): Refers to God's faithful followers.

- υ□ δωρ πολύς (Strong's G5204, G4183): Symbolizes a powerful and overwhelming sound.

- βροντη□ μεγα□ λη (Strong's G1027, G3173): Indicates the powerful voice of God.

- γα□ μος τοῦ ἀρνίου (Strong's G1062, G721): Symbolizes the union of Christ and His Church.

- γυνη□ (Strong's G1135): Represents the Church, the bride of Christ.

- βυ□ σσινος λαμπρο□ ς καθαρο□ ς (Strong's G1039, G2986, G2513): Symbolizes purity and righteousness.

- δικαι□ ωμα (Strong's G1345): Represents the deeds of the saints.

- μακα□ ριος (Strong's G3107): Indicates a state of happiness and favor.

- δεῖπνον γάμος (Strong's G1173, G1062): Represents the celebratory feast of the union between Christ and His Church.

- μαρτυρι□ α Ἰησοῦς (Strong's G3141, G2424): Refers to the witness and proclamation of Jesus.

- πνεῦμα προφητεία (Strong's G4151, G4394): Indicates the Holy Spirit's role in revealing and testifying about Jesus.

- λευκο□ς □ππος (Strong's G3022, G2462): Symbolizes victory and purity.

- πιστο□ς και□ αληθινός (Strong's G4103, G228): Indicates Jesus' reliability and truthfulness.

- φλο□ξ πῦρ (Strong's G5395, G4442): Represents penetrating judgment.

- πολυ□ς διάδημα (Strong's G4183, G1238): Symbolizes supreme authority and kingship.

- λο□γος τοῦ Θεοῦ (Strong's G3056, G2316): Identifies Jesus as the divine Logos.

- στρατευ□ματα ο' ουρανός (Strong's G4753, G3772): Represents the heavenly hosts.

- ρομφαι□α οξύς (Strong's G4501, G3691): Symbolizes the power of Jesus' word.

- ράβδος σιδηροῦς (Strong's G4464, G4603): Represents Jesus' strong and just rule.

- ληνο□ς οργή (Strong's G3025, G3709): Symbolizes the execution of divine judgment.

- βασιλευ□ς βασιλέων και□ κύριος κυρίων (Strong's G935, G935, G2962, G2962): Emphasizes Jesus' supreme authority over all rulers.

- αἴγγελος (Strong's G32): Represents a messenger of God.

- δεῖπνον ὁ μεγάλος Θεός (Strong's G1173, G3173, G2316): Symbolizes the divine retribution against God's enemies.

- θηρίον (Strong's G2342): Represents the oppressive and blasphemous political power.

- ψευδοπροφήτης (Strong's G5578): Represents the deceptive religious leader.

- λίμνη πῦρ (Strong's G3041, G4442): Symbolizes the final destination of judgment and eternal punishment.

- ρομφαία ἐκ ὁ στόμα (Strong's G4501, G1537, G3588, G4750): Represents the power of Jesus' word to execute judgment.

Practical Application

The vision of the triumph of Jesus in Revelation 19 holds timeless relevance for believers today. Key lessons include:

1. Recognizing Jesus' Authority: The depiction of Jesus as the rider on the white horse emphasizes His supreme authority and kingship. Believers are called to recognize and submit to His lordship.

2. Understanding the Justice of God's Judgments: The praise of the heavenly multitude highlights the fairness and

righteousness of God's judgments. Believers can trust in God's justice and His ultimate victory over evil.

3. Participating in the Marriage Supper of the Lamb: The celebration of the marriage supper symbolizes the joyous union between Christ and His Church. Believers are encouraged to live in readiness for this divine union, adorned in the righteousness of the saints.

4. Enduring with Faith: The vision of Jesus' triumph and the defeat of the beast and the false prophet provide assurance of God's ultimate victory. Believers are called to endure with faith, knowing that Jesus will overcome all forces of evil.

5. Living as Faithful Witnesses: The emphasis on the testimony of Jesus and the spirit of prophecy encourages believers to live as faithful witnesses, proclaiming the truth and standing firm in their faith.

Conclusion

The vision of the triumph of Jesus in Revelation 19 provides a profound depiction of His victory and authority over all forces of evil. Through the imagery of the heavenly multitude's praise, the marriage supper of the Lamb, the rider on the white horse, and the defeat of the beast and the false prophet, believers are called to recognize Jesus' authority, understand the justice of God's judgments, participate in the divine union with Christ, endure with faith, and live as faithful witnesses. By examining these verses through an expository study with exhaustive Strong's Concordance, we uncover the depth of this vision and its enduring relevance for the church today. As we embrace the truths revealed in the triumph of Jesus, we will be drawn into deeper worship and greater readiness to stand firm in our faith.

CHAPTER 13

THE MILLENNIUM REIGN

Revelation 20 outlines the thousand-year reign of Jesus, often referred to as the Millennium. During this period, Satan is bound, and righteousness prevails under Jesus' authority. This chapter highlights Jesus' power to restore peace and justice to the world, providing a glimpse of His ultimate kingdom. By examining these verses through an expository study with exhaustive Strong's Concordance, we can uncover the deeper meanings and significant truths revealed in this vision.

The Binding of Satan

Revelation 20:1-3 describes the binding of Satan:

> "Then I saw an angel coming down from heaven, having the key to the bottomless pit and a great chain in his hand. He laid hold of the dragon, that serpent of old, who is the Devil and Satan, and bound him for a thousand years; and he cast him into the bottomless pit, and shut him up, and set a seal on him, so that he should deceive the nations no more till the thousand years were finished. But after these things he must be released for a little while."

- Angel (ἄγγελος - Strong's G32): Represents a messenger of God.

- Key to the Bottomless Pit (κλεὶς ἄβυσσος - Strong's G2807, G12): Symbolizes authority over the abyss.

- Great Chain (μέγας ἅλυσις - Strong's G3173, G254): Represents the power to restrain Satan.

- Dragon, Serpent, Devil, Satan (δράκων, ὄφις, διάβολος, Σατανᾶς - Strong's G1404, G3789, G1228, G4567): Different names emphasizing the evil nature of Satan.

- Bound for a Thousand Years (δέω χίλιοι ἔτος - Strong's G1210, G5507, G2094): Indicates a prolonged period of restraint.

- Bottomless Pit (α□βυσσος - Strong's G12): Represents the abyss or the realm of the dead.

- Seal (σφραγι□ζω - Strong's G4972): Signifies security and the prevention of escape.

The binding of Satan signifies the restriction of his influence and deception over the nations. The angel, possessing the key and chain, demonstrates God's authority to imprison Satan for a thousand years, symbolizing a period of peace and righteousness.

The Reign of the Saints

Revelation 20:4-6 describes the reign of the saints with Christ:

> "And I saw thrones, and they sat on them, and judgment was committed to them. Then I saw the souls of those who had been beheaded for their witness to Jesus and for the word of God, who had not worshiped the beast or his image, and had not received his mark on their foreheads or on their hands. And they lived and reigned with Christ for a thousand years. But the rest of the dead did not live again until the thousand years were finished. This is the first resurrection. Blessed and holy is he who has part in the first resurrection. Over such the second death has no power, but they shall be priests of God and of Christ, and shall reign with Him a thousand years."

- Thrones (θρο□νος - Strong's G2362): Symbolize authority and judgment.

- Souls of the Beheaded (ψυχη□ ἀποκεφαλίζω - Strong's G5590, G3990): Represents the martyrs for Jesus.

- Witness to Jesus (μαρτυρι□α Ἰησοῦς - Strong's G3141, G2424): Indicates the testimony and proclamation of Jesus.

- Beast and His Image (θηρι□ον και□ εἰκών - Strong's G2342, G1504): Represents the Antichrist and idolatry.

- First Resurrection (πρῶτος ἀνάστασις - Strong's G4413, G386): Indicates the resurrection of the righteous.

- Second Death (δευ□τερος θα□νατος - Strong's G1208, G2288): Represents eternal separation from God.

- Priests of God and Christ (ἱερεύς τοῦ Θεοῦ και□ Χριστός - Strong's G2409, G2316, G5547): Symbolizes a holy and dedicated service to God.

The saints who have been faithful to Jesus and resisted the beast are resurrected to reign with Christ for a thousand years. This period, known as the first resurrection, is marked by blessing and holiness, with the saints serving as priests and rulers in Christ's kingdom.

The Release and Final Defeat of Satan

Revelation 20:7-10 describes Satan's release and ultimate defeat:

> "Now when the thousand years have expired, Satan will be released from his prison and will go out to deceive the nations which are in the four corners of the earth, Gog and Magog, to gather them together to battle, whose number is as the sand of the sea. They went up on the breadth of the earth and surrounded the camp of the saints and the beloved city. And fire came down from God out of heaven and devoured them. The devil, who deceived them, was cast into the lake of fire and brimstone where the beast and the false prophet are. And they will be tormented day and night forever and ever."

- Expired (τελε□ω - Strong's G5055): Indicates the completion of a period.

- Released (λυ□ω - Strong's G3089): Represents the loosening or freeing of Satan.

- Four Corners of the Earth (τε□σσαρες γωνία ὁ γῆ - Strong's G5064, G1137, G1093): Symbolizes the entire world.

- Gog and Magog (Γω□γ και□ Μάγωγ - Strong's G1136, G3098): Represents the nations in rebellion against God.

- Camp of the Saints (παρεμβολη□ ὁ α□γιος - Strong's G3925, G40): Indicates the dwelling place of God's people.

- Beloved City (ἀγαπάω πόλις - Strong's G25, G4172): Represents Jerusalem, the city of God's favor.

- Lake of Fire (λίμνη πῦρ - Strong's G3041, G4442): Symbolizes the place of eternal punishment.

- Tormented (βασανίζω - Strong's G928): Indicates continuous suffering.

After the thousand years, Satan is briefly released to deceive the nations once more. This final rebellion, involving Gog and Magog, ends with God's decisive intervention, sending fire from heaven to devour the enemies. Satan is then cast into the lake of fire, where he will be tormented forever, marking his ultimate defeat.

The Great White Throne Judgment

Revelation 20:11-15 describes the final judgment before the great white throne:

> "Then I saw a great white throne and Him who sat on it, from whose face the earth and the heaven fled away. And there was found no place for them. And I saw the dead, small and great, standing before God, and books were opened. And another book was opened, which is the Book of Life. And the dead were judged according to their works, by the things which were written in the books. The sea gave up the dead who were in it, and Death and Hades delivered up the dead who were in them. And they were judged, each one according to his works. Then Death and Hades were cast into the lake of fire. This is the second death. And anyone not

found written in the Book of Life was cast into the lake of fire."

- Great White Throne (με□γας λευκο□ς θρόνος - Strong's G3173, G3022, G2362): Symbolizes purity and divine judgment.

- Earth and Heaven Fled (γῆ και□ ουρανός φεύγω - Strong's G1093, G2532, G3772, G5343): Represents the dissolution of the current order.

- Books (βι□βλος - Strong's G976): Represents records of deeds and actions.

- Book of Life (βι□βλος ζωη□ - Strong's G976, G2222): Symbolizes the record of those who belong to Christ.

- Judged According to Their Works (κρι□νω κατα□ ε□ργον - Strong's G2919, G2596, G2041): Indicates accountability for actions.

- Death and Hades (θα□νατος και□ α□δης - Strong's G2288, G86): Represents the final enemies.

- Second Death (δευ□τερος θα□νατος - Strong's G1208, G2288): Represents eternal separation from God.

The great white throne judgment marks the final and ultimate judgment of all humanity. The dead, both small and great, are judged according to their works recorded in the books. Those not found in the Book of Life are cast into the lake of fire, symbolizing the second death and eternal separation from God.

Expository Insights

Examining the text through exhaustive Strong's Concordance reveals deeper meanings and connections:

- α□γγελος (Strong's G32): Represents a messenger of God.

- κλει□ς α□βυσσος (Strong's G2807, G12): Symbolizes authority over the abyss.

- με□γας α□λυσις (Strong's G3173, G254): Represents the power to restrain Satan.

- δρα□κων, ο□φις, διάβολος, Σατανᾶς (Strong's G1404, G3789, G1228, G4567): Different names emphasizing the evil nature of Satan.

- δε□ω χίλιοι ε□τος (Strong's G1210, G5507, G2094): Indicates a prolonged period of restraint.

- σφραγι□ζω (Strong's G4972): Signifies security and the prevention of escape.

- θρο□νος (Strong's G2362): Symbolize authority and judgment.

- ψυχη□ ἀποκεφαλίζω (Strong's G5590, G3990): Represents the martyrs for Jesus.

- μαρτυρι□α Ἰησοῦς (Strong's G3141, G2424): Indicates the testimony and proclamation of Jesus.

- θηρι□ ον και□ εἰκών (Strong's G2342, G1504): Represents the Antichrist and idolatry.

- πρῶτος ἀνάστασις (Strong's G4413, G386): Indicates the resurrection of the righteous.

- δευ□ τερος θα□ νατος (Strong's G1208, G2288): Represents eternal separation from God.

- ἱερεύς τοῦ Θεοῦ και□ Χριστός (Strong's G2409, G2316, G5547): Symbolizes a holy and dedicated service to God.

- τελε□ ω (Strong's G5055): Indicates the completion of a period.

- λυ□ ω (Strong's G3089): Represents the loosening or freeing of Satan.

- τε□ σσαρες γωνία ὁ γῆ (Strong's G5064, G1137, G1093): Symbolizes the entire world.

- Γω□ γ και□ Μάγωγ (Strong's G1136, G3098): Represents the nations in rebellion against God.

- παρεμβολη□ ὁ α□ γιος (Strong's G3925, G40): Indicates the dwelling place of God's people.

- ἀγαπάω πόλις (Strong's G25, G4172): Represents Jerusalem, the city of God's favor.

- λι□ μνη πῦρ (Strong's G3041, G4442): Symbolizes the place of eternal punishment.

- βασανι□ζω (Strong's G928): Indicates continuous suffering.

- με□γας λευκο□ς θρόνος (Strong's G3173, G3022, G2362): Symbolizes purity and divine judgment.

- γῆ και□ ουρανός φεύγω (Strong's G1093, G2532, G3772, G5343): Represents the dissolution of the current order.

- βι□βλος (Strong's G976): Represents records of deeds and actions.

- βι□βλος ζωη□ (Strong's G976, G2222): Symbolizes the record of those who belong to Christ.

- κρι□νω κατα□ ε□ργον (Strong's G2919, G2596, G2041): Indicates accountability for actions.

- θα□νατος και□ α□δης (Strong's G2288, G86): Represents the final enemies.

- δευ□τερος θα□νατος (Strong's G1208, G2288): Represents eternal separation from God.

Practical Application

The vision of the Millennium Reign in Revelation 20 holds timeless relevance for believers today. Key lessons include:

1. Recognizing Jesus' Authority: The binding of Satan and the reign of the saints with Christ emphasize Jesus'

supreme authority and His power to establish righteousness. Believers are called to recognize and submit to His lordship.

2. Understanding the Justice of God's Judgments: The final defeat of Satan and the great white throne judgment highlight the fairness and righteousness of God's judgments. Believers can trust in God's justice and His ultimate victory over evil.

3. Living in Readiness for the Resurrection: The first resurrection represents the hope of eternal life for the righteous. Believers are encouraged to live in readiness for this divine promise, adorned in righteousness and faithfulness.

4. Enduring with Faith: The period of Satan's binding and subsequent release calls believers to endure with faith, knowing that Jesus will ultimately overcome all forces of evil and establish His kingdom.

5. Living as Faithful Witnesses: The emphasis on the testimony of Jesus and the reign of the saints encourages believers to live as faithful witnesses, proclaiming the truth and standing firm in their faith.

Conclusion

The vision of the Millennium Reign in Revelation 20 provides a profound depiction of Jesus' authority and power to establish righteousness and justice. Through the imagery of the binding of Satan, the reign of the saints, the final defeat of

Satan, and the great white throne judgment, believers are called to recognize Jesus' authority, understand the justice of God's judgments, live in readiness for the resurrection, endure with faith, and live as faithful witnesses. By examining these verses through an expository study with exhaustive Strong's Concordance, we uncover the depth of this vision and its enduring relevance for the church today. As we embrace the truths revealed in the Millennium Reign, we will be drawn into deeper worship and greater readiness to stand firm in our faith.

CHAPTER 14

THE FINAL JUDGMENT

The great white throne judgment in Revelation 20:11-15 reveals Jesus as the ultimate judge of all humanity. His judgment is just and final, separating the righteous from the wicked and establishing eternal destinies. By examining these verses through an expository study with exhaustive Strong's Concordance, we can uncover the deeper meanings and significant truths revealed in this vision.

The Great White Throne

Revelation 20:11 introduces the great white throne:

> "Then I saw a great white throne and Him who sat on it, from whose face the earth and the heaven fled away. And there was found no place for them."

- Great White Throne (μέγας λευκός θρόνος - Strong's G3173, G3022, G2362): Symbolizes purity, majesty, and divine judgment.

- Him Who Sat on It (καθῆμαι - Strong's G2521): Refers to Jesus as the judge.

- Earth and Heaven Fled Away (φεύγω γῆ καί οὐρανός - Strong's G5343, G1093, G2532, G3772): Represents the dissolution of the current order of creation.

The great white throne signifies the purity and majesty of divine judgment. The fleeing of the earth and heaven emphasizes the all-encompassing and transformative nature of this judgment.

The Books and the Book of Life

Revelation 20:12-13 describes the opening of the books and the Book of Life:

> "And I saw the dead, small and great, standing before God, and books were opened. And another book was opened, which is the Book of Life. And the dead were judged according to their works, by the things which were written in the books. The sea gave up the dead who were in it, and Death and Hades delivered up the dead who were in them. And they were judged, each one according to his works."

- The Dead, Small and Great (νεκρο□ ς μικρός και□ μεγάς - Strong's G3498, G3398, G2532, G3173): Represents all people regardless of status.

- Standing Before God (ἐ□ στηκα ἐνώπιον ὁ Θεός - Strong's G2476, G1799, G3588, G2316): Indicates readiness for judgment.

- Books (βι□ βλος - Strong's G976): Represents the records of deeds and actions.

- Book of Life (βι□ βλος ζωη□ - Strong's G976, G2222): Symbolizes the record of those who belong to Christ.

- Judged According to Their Works (κρι□ νω κατα□ ε□ ργον - Strong's G2919, G2596, G2041): Indicates accountability for actions.

- Sea, Death, and Hades (θα□ λασσα, θάνατος, α□ ͅδης - Strong's G2281, G2288, G86): Represents the entirety of the dead from all realms.

The opening of the books and the Book of Life signifies the comprehensive and meticulous nature of God's judgment. The dead are judged according to their works, emphasizing the accountability of each person before God.

The Second Death

Revelation 20:14-15 describes the second death and the final destiny of those not found in the Book of Life:

> "Then Death and Hades were cast into the lake of fire. This is the second death. And anyone not found written in the Book of Life was cast into the lake of fire."

- Death and Hades (θα□νατος και□ α□,δης - Strong's G2288, G86): Represents the final enemies.

- Lake of Fire (λι□μνη πῦρ - Strong's G3041, G4442): Symbolizes the place of eternal punishment.

- Second Death (δευ□τερος θα□νατος - Strong's G1208, G2288): Represents eternal separation from God.

The casting of Death and Hades into the lake of fire signifies the ultimate defeat of the final enemies. The second death represents eternal separation from God, reserved for those not found in the Book of Life.

Expository Insights

Examining the text through exhaustive Strong's Concordance reveals deeper meanings and connections:

- μέγας λευκὸς θρόνος (Strong's G3173, G3022, G2362): Symbolizes purity, majesty, and divine judgment.

- καθῆμαι (Strong's G2521): Refers to Jesus as the judge.

- φεύγω γῆ καὶ οὐρανός (Strong's G5343, G1093, G2532, G3772): Represents the dissolution of the current order of creation.

- νεκρὸς μικρὸς καὶ μεγάς (Strong's G3498, G3398, G2532, G3173): Represents all people regardless of status.

- ἕστηκα ἐνώπιον ὁ Θεός (Strong's G2476, G1799, G3588, G2316): Indicates readiness for judgment.

- βίβλος (Strong's G976): Represents the records of deeds and actions.

- βίβλος ζωῆ (Strong's G976, G2222): Symbolizes the record of those who belong to Christ.

- κρίνω κατὰ ἔργον (Strong's G2919, G2596, G2041): Indicates accountability for actions.

- θάλασσα, θάνατος, ἅδης (Strong's G2281, G2288, G86): Represents the entirety of the dead from all realms.

- λίμνη πῦρ (Strong's G3041, G4442): Symbolizes the place of eternal punishment.

- δεύτερος θάνατος (Strong's G1208, G2288): Represents eternal separation from God.

Practical Application

The vision of the final judgment in Revelation 20:11-15 holds timeless relevance for believers today. Key lessons include:

1. Recognizing Jesus' Authority: The depiction of Jesus as the judge on the great white throne emphasizes His supreme authority and power to execute judgment. Believers are called to recognize and submit to His lordship.

2. Understanding the Justice of God's Judgments: The comprehensive nature of the judgment, with books recording deeds and the Book of Life, highlights the fairness and righteousness of God's judgments. Believers can trust in God's justice and His ultimate victory over evil.

3. Living in Readiness for Judgment: The vision of the final judgment calls believers to live in readiness, knowing that they will be held accountable for their actions. Believers are encouraged to live righteous and faithful lives.

4. Finding Assurance in the Book of Life: The presence of the Book of Life provides assurance for believers, knowing that their names are recorded in it through faith in Christ. This assurance motivates believers to persevere in their faith.

5. Enduring with Faith: The final judgment and the defeat of Death and Hades call believers to endure with faith,

knowing that Jesus will ultimately overcome all forces of evil and establish His kingdom.

Conclusion

The vision of the final judgment in Revelation 20:11-15 provides a profound depiction of Jesus' authority and power to execute just and final judgment. Through the imagery of the great white throne, the opening of the books and the Book of Life, and the casting of Death and Hades into the lake of fire, believers are called to recognize Jesus' authority, understand the justice of God's judgments, live in readiness for judgment, find assurance in the Book of Life, and endure with faith. By examining these verses through an expository study with exhaustive Strong's Concordance, we uncover the depth of this vision and its enduring relevance for the church today. As we embrace the truths revealed in the final judgment, we will be drawn into deeper worship and greater readiness to stand firm in our faith.

CHAPTER 15

THE NEW HEAVEN AND NEW EARTH

Revelation 21-22 presents a breathtaking vision of the new heaven and new earth, where Jesus reigns eternally with His people. This vision signifies the culmination of God's redemptive plan through Jesus, who declares, "Behold, I make all things new" (Revelation 21:5). By examining these chapters through an expository study with exhaustive Strong's

Concordance, we can uncover the profound meanings and significant truths revealed in this ultimate fulfillment of God's promise.

The New Heaven and New Earth

Revelation 21:1-4 introduces the new heaven and new earth:

> "Now I saw a new heaven and a new earth, for the first heaven and the first earth had passed away. Also there was no more sea. Then I, John, saw the holy city, New Jerusalem, coming down out of heaven from God, prepared as a bride adorned for her husband. And I heard a loud voice from heaven saying, 'Behold, the tabernacle of God is with men, and He will dwell with them, and they shall be His people. God Himself will be with them and be their God. And God will wipe away every tear from their eyes; there shall be no more death, nor sorrow, nor crying. There shall be no more pain, for the former things have passed away.'"

- New Heaven and New Earth (καινο□ ς ουρανός και□ καινο□ ς γῆ - Strong's G2537, G3772, G2537, G1093): Represents the renewed creation.

- First Heaven and First Earth Passed Away (πρῶτος ουρανός και□ πρῶτος γῆ παρέρχομαι - Strong's G4413, G3772, G4413, G1093, G3928): Indicates the end of the old order.

- No More Sea (θα□λασσα οὐκέτι ἐ□στιν - Strong's G2281, G3765, G2076): Symbolizes the removal of chaos and separation.

- Holy City, New Jerusalem (α□γιος πόλις, καινο□ς Ἱερουσαλήμ - Strong's G40, G4172, G2537, G2419): Represents the dwelling place of God with His people.

- Tabernacle of God (σκηνη□ ὁ Θεός - Strong's G4633, G3588, G2316): Symbolizes God's presence with humanity.

- Wipe Away Every Tear (ἐξαλείφω πᾶς δάκρυον - Strong's G1813, G3956, G1144): Indicates the end of suffering and sorrow.

- No More Death, Sorrow, Crying, Pain (θα□νατος, πένθος, κραυγή, πόνος οὐκέτι ἐ□στιν - Strong's G2288, G3997, G2906, G4192, G3765, G2076): Represents the complete removal of all forms of suffering.

The vision of the new heaven and new earth signifies the renewal of creation and the end of the old order marked by pain, sorrow, and death. The New Jerusalem, descending from heaven, symbolizes the perfect union between God and His people, where He dwells with them and wipes away every tear, signifying the end of all suffering.

Jesus Declares All Things New

Revelation 21:5-8 highlights Jesus' declaration of making all things new:

> "Then He who sat on the throne said, 'Behold, I make all things new.' And He said to me, 'Write, for these words are true and faithful.' And He said to me, 'It is done! I am the Alpha and the Omega, the Beginning and the End. I will give of the fountain of the water of life freely to him who thirsts. He who overcomes shall inherit all things, and I will be his God and he shall be My son. But the cowardly, unbelieving, abominable, murderers, sexually immoral, sorcerers, idolaters, and all liars shall have their part in the lake which burns with fire and brimstone, which is the second death.'"

- Make All Things New (καινο□ ς ποιέω πᾶς - Strong's G2537, G4160, G3956): Indicates the renewal and transformation of creation.

- True and Faithful (αληθινός και□ πιστός - Strong's G228, G4103): Emphasizes the reliability and trustworthiness of God's words.

- It Is Done (γε□ γονα - Strong's G1096): Indicates the completion of God's plan.

- Alpha and Omega (Αλφα και□ Ω'μέγα - Strong's G1, G5598): Represent Jesus as the beginning and the end.

- Water of Life (ὕδωρ ζωή - Strong's G5204, G2222): Symbolizes the gift of eternal life.

- Overcomes (νικάω - Strong's G3528): Refers to those who remain faithful and victorious.

- Lake of Fire and Brimstone (λίμνη πῦρ καὶ θεῖον - Strong's G3041, G4442, G2303): Represents the place of eternal punishment.

- Second Death (δεύτερος θάνατος - Strong's G1208, G2288): Indicates eternal separation from God.

Jesus' declaration of making all things new signifies the complete renewal of creation and the fulfillment of God's redemptive plan. His promise of the water of life to those who thirst and the inheritance for those who overcome emphasizes the blessings for the faithful, while the warning of the second death highlights the consequences for the wicked.

The New Jerusalem

Revelation 21:9-21 describes the New Jerusalem:

> "Then one of the seven angels who had the seven bowls filled with the seven last plagues came to me and talked with me, saying, 'Come, I will show you the bride, the Lamb's wife.' And he carried me away in the Spirit to a great and high mountain, and showed me the great city, the holy Jerusalem, descending out of heaven from God, having the glory of God. Her light was like a most precious stone, like a jasper stone,

clear as crystal. Also she had a great and high wall with twelve gates, and twelve angels at the gates, and names written on them, which are the names of the twelve tribes of the children of Israel: three gates on the east, three gates on the north, three gates on the south, and three gates on the west. Now the wall of the city had twelve foundations, and on them were the names of the twelve apostles of the Lamb. And he who talked with me had a gold reed to measure the city, its gates, and its wall. The city is laid out as a square; its length is as great as its breadth. And he measured the city with the reed: twelve thousand furlongs. Its length, breadth, and height are equal. Then he measured its wall: one hundred and forty-four cubits, according to the measure of a man, that is, of an angel. The construction of its wall was of jasper; and the city was pure gold, like clear glass. The foundations of the wall of the city were adorned with all kinds of precious stones: the first foundation was jasper, the second sapphire, the third chalcedony, the fourth emerald, the fifth sardonyx, the sixth sardius, the seventh chrysolite, the eighth beryl, the ninth topaz, the tenth chrysoprase, the eleventh jacinth, and the twelfth amethyst. The twelve gates were twelve pearls: each individual gate was of one pearl. And the street of the city was pure gold, like transparent glass."

- Bride, the Lamb's Wife (νυ□μφη ἀμνός - Strong's G3565, G721): Symbolizes the Church, the bride of Christ.

- Great and High Mountain (με□γας και□ ὑψηλός ο□ρος - Strong's G3173, G5308, G3735): Represents a place of revelation and vision.

- Holy Jerusalem (α□γιος Ἰερουσαλήμ - Strong's G40, G2419): Represents the dwelling place of God with His people.

- Glory of God (δο□ξα ὁ Θεός - Strong's G1391, G3588, G2316): Indicates the divine presence.

- Twelve Gates, Twelve Tribes (δω□δεκα πυλω□ν, δω□δεκα φυλη□ - Strong's G1427, G4440, G1427, G5443): Represents the inclusion of all God's people.

- Twelve Foundations, Twelve Apostles (δω□δεκα θεμέλιος, δώδεκα ἀπόστολος - Strong's G1427, G2310, G1427, G652): Symbolizes the foundation of the Church.

- Gold Reed (χρυσο□ς καλα□μη - Strong's G5557, G2563): Represents the standard of measurement.

- Jasper, Sapphire, Chalcedony, Emerald (ἰάσπιδι, σάπφιρος, χαλκηδών, σμάραγδος - Strong's G2393, G4552, G5472, G4665): Represents the beauty and preciousness of the city.

- Pure Gold, Transparent Glass (χρυσο□ς καθαρός, ὑάλινος - Strong's G5553, G2513, G5194): Symbolizes purity and clarity.

The detailed description of the New Jerusalem emphasizes its beauty, holiness, and perfection. The twelve gates and foundations symbolize the inclusivity and foundation of God's people, while the precious materials highlight the city's divine glory and splendor.

The Temple and the Light

Revelation 21:22-27 describes the absence of a temple and the presence of God's light:

> "But I saw no temple in it, for the Lord God Almighty and the Lamb are its temple. The city had no need of the sun or of the moon to shine in it, for the glory of God illuminated it. The Lamb is its light. And the nations of those who are saved shall walk in its light, and the kings of the earth bring their glory and honor into it. Its gates shall not be shut at all by day (there shall be no night there). And they shall bring the glory and the honor of the nations into it. But there shall by no means enter it anything that defiles, or causes an abomination or a lie, but only those who are written in the Lamb's Book of Life."

- No Temple (οὐκ ἱερόν - Strong's G3756, G2411): Indicates direct access to God's presence.

- Lord God Almighty and the Lamb (Κυ□ριος Θεός Παντοκράτωρ και□ ἀμνός - Strong's G2962, G2316, G3841, G2532, G721): Represent the divine presence as the temple.

- Glory of God (δο□ξα ὁ Θεός - Strong's G1391, G3588, G2316): Indicates divine illumination.

- Lamb is its Light (ἀμνός φάος - Strong's G721, G5457): Symbolizes Jesus as the source of light.

- Nations Walk in its Light (ε□θνος περιπατέω φάος - Strong's G1484, G4043, G5457): Represents the inclusion of all peoples in God's kingdom.

- Lamb's Book of Life (βι□βλος ζωή ὁ ἀμνός - Strong's G976, G2222, G3588, G721): Symbolizes the record of those who belong to Christ.

The absence of a temple in the New Jerusalem signifies direct access to God's presence, with the Lord God Almighty and the Lamb as its temple. The divine illumination by God's glory and the Lamb as the light emphasize the perfect and eternal presence of God. The inclusion of all nations and the exclusion of anything impure highlight the purity and inclusivity of God's eternal kingdom.

The River of Life and the Tree of Life

Revelation 22:1-5 describes the river of life and the tree of life:

> "And he showed me a pure river of water of life, clear as crystal, proceeding from the throne of God and of the Lamb. In the middle of its street, and on either side of the river, was the tree of life, which bore twelve fruits, each tree yielding its fruit every month. The leaves of the tree were for the healing of the nations. And there shall be no more curse, but the throne of God and of the Lamb shall be in it, and His servants shall serve Him. They shall see His face, and His name shall be on their foreheads. There shall be no night there: They need no lamp nor light of the sun, for the Lord God gives them light. And they shall reign forever and ever."

- Pure River of Water of Life (καθαρο□ς ποταμός υ□δωρ ζωή - Strong's G2513, G4215, G5204, G2222): Symbolizes the source of eternal life.

- Throne of God and of the Lamb (θρο□νος ὁ Θεός και□ ἀμνός - Strong's G2362, G3588, G2316, G2532, G721): Represents divine authority and presence.

- Tree of Life (ξυ□λον ζωη□ - Strong's G3586, G2222): Symbolizes eternal life and healing.

- Healing of the Nations (θεραπευ□ω ε□θνος - Strong's G2322, G1484): Indicates the restoration and wholeness of all peoples.

- No More Curse (οὐκέτι κατάθεμα - Strong's G3765, G2652): Represents the end of the curse of sin.

- See His Face (ὁράω αὐτός πρόσωπον - Strong's G3708, G846, G4383): Indicates direct vision of God's presence.

- Name on Their Foreheads (ο□ νομα αὐτός μέτωπον - Strong's G3686, G846, G3359): Symbolizes belonging and identity in God.

The river of life and the tree of life symbolize the abundance and continuity of eternal life. The healing of the nations, the end of the curse, and the direct vision of God's face emphasize the complete restoration and perfect fellowship with God. The eternal reign of the saints highlights the everlasting nature of God's kingdom.

Expository Insights

Examining the text through exhaustive Strong's Concordance reveals deeper meanings and connections:

- καινο□ ς οὐρανός και□ καινο□ ς γῆ (Strong's G2537, G3772, G2537, G1093): Represents the renewed creation.

- πρῶτος οὐρανός και□ πρῶτος γῆ παρέρχομαι (Strong's G4413, G3772, G4413, G1093, G3928): Indicates the end of the old order.

- θα□ λασσα οὐκέτι ε□ στιν (Strong's G2281, G3765, G2076): Symbolizes the removal of chaos and separation.

- α□γιος πόλις, καινο□ς Ίερουσαλήμ (Strong's G40, G4172, G2537, G2419): Represents the dwelling place of God with His people.

- σκηνη□ ο Θεός (Strong's G4633, G3588, G2316): Symbolizes God's presence with humanity.

- εξαλείφω πᾶς δάκρυον (Strong's G1813, G3956, G1144): Indicates the end of suffering and sorrow.

- θα□νατος, πένθος, κραυγή, πόνος ουκέτι ε□στιν (Strong's G2288, G3997, G2906, G4192, G3765, G2076): Represents the complete removal of all forms of suffering.

- καινο□ς ποιέω πᾶς (Strong's G2537, G4160, G3956): Indicates the renewal and transformation of creation.

- αληθινός και□ πιστός (Strong's G228, G4103): Emphasizes the reliability and trustworthiness of God's words.

- γε□γονα (Strong's G1096): Indicates the completion of God's plan.

- Αλφα και□ Ωμέγα (Strong's G1, G5598): Represents Jesus as the beginning and the end.

- υ□δωρ ζωή (Strong's G5204, G2222): Symbolizes the gift of eternal life.

- νικα□ω (Strong's G3528): Refers to those who remain faithful and victorious.

- λι□μνη πῦρ καὶ□ θεῖον (Strong's G3041, G4442, G2303): Represents the place of eternal punishment.

- δευ□τερος θα□νατος (Strong's G1208, G2288): Indicates eternal separation from God.

- νυ□μφη ἀμνός (Strong's G3565, G721): Symbolizes the Church, the bride of Christ.

- με□γας καὶ□ ὑψηλός ο□ρος (Strong's G3173, G5308, G3735): Represents a place of revelation and vision.

- δο□ξα ὁ Θεός (Strong's G1391, G3588, G2316): Indicates the divine presence.

- δω□δεκα πυλω□ν, δω□δεκα φυλη□ (Strong's G1427, G4440, G1427, G5443): Represents the inclusion of all God's people.

- δω□δεκα θεμέλιος, δώδεκα ἀπόστολος (Strong's G1427, G2310, G1427, G652): Symbolizes the foundation of the Church.

- χρυσο□ς καλα□μη (Strong's G5557, G2563): Represents the standard of measurement.

- ἰάσπιδι, σάπφιρος, χαλκηδών, σμάραγδος (Strong's G2393, G4552, G5472, G4665): Represents the beauty and preciousness of the city.

- χρυσο□ς καθαρός, ὑάλινος (Strong's G5553, G2513, G5194): Symbolizes purity and clarity.

- οὐκ ἱερόν (Strong's G3756, G2411): Indicates direct access to God's presence.

- Κυ□ριος Θεός Παντοκράτωρ καὶ□ ἀμνός (Strong's G2962, G2316, G3841, G2532, G721): Represent the divine presence as the temple.

- ἀμνός φάος (Strong's G721, G5457): Symbolizes Jesus as the source of light.

- ἐ□θνος περιπατέω φάος (Strong's G1484, G4043, G5457): Represents the inclusion of all peoples in God's kingdom.

- βι□βλος ζωή ὁ ἀμνός (Strong's G976, G2222, G3588, G721): Symbolizes the record of those who belong to Christ.

- καθαρο□ς ποταμός ὕ□δωρ ζωή (Strong's G2513, G4215, G5204, G2222): Symbolizes the source of eternal life.

- θρο□νος ὁ Θεός καὶ□ ἀμνός (Strong's G2362, G3588, G2316, G2532, G721): Represents divine authority and presence.

- ξυ□λον ζωη□ (Strong's G3586, G2222): Symbolizes eternal life and healing.

- θεραπευ□ω ἐ□θνος (Strong's G2322, G1484): Indicates the restoration and wholeness of all peoples.

- οὐκέτι κατάθεμα (Strong's G3765, G2652): Represents the end of the curse of sin.

- ὁράω αὐτός πρόσωπον (Strong's G3708, G846, G4383): Indicates direct vision of God's presence.

- o□νομα αὐτός μέτωπον (Strong's G3686, G846, G3359): Symbolizes belonging and identity in God.

Practical Application

The vision of the new heaven and new earth in Revelation 21-22 holds timeless relevance for believers today. Key lessons include:

1. Recognizing the Fulfillment of God's Promise: The vision signifies the ultimate fulfillment of God's redemptive plan, emphasizing His faithfulness and the assurance of His promises.

2. Living in Anticipation of Eternal Life: The description of the New Jerusalem and the removal of all suffering encourages believers to live in anticipation of the eternal life promised by God.

3. Embracing God's Presence: The absence of a temple and the direct access to God's presence highlight the importance of cultivating a close and personal relationship with God.

4. Finding Assurance in God's Plan: The declaration of making all things new provides assurance that God is in control and will bring about the complete renewal of creation.

5. Living as Faithful Witnesses: The emphasis on the Lamb's Book of Life and the inheritance for those who overcome encourages believers to live as faithful witnesses, remaining steadfast in their faith.

Conclusion

The vision of the new heaven and new earth in Revelation 21-22 provides a profound depiction of the ultimate fulfillment of God's redemptive plan and the eternal reign of Jesus with His people. Through the imagery of the New Jerusalem, the river of life, the tree of life, and the absence of a temple, believers are called to recognize the fulfillment of God's promise, live in anticipation of eternal life, embrace God's presence, find assurance in God's plan, and live as faithful witnesses. By examining these verses through an expository study with exhaustive Strong's Concordance, we uncover the depth of this vision and its enduring relevance for the church today. As we embrace the truths revealed in the new heaven and new earth, we will be drawn into deeper worship and greater readiness to stand firm in our faith.

CHAPTER 16

THE ETERNAL SOVEREIGNTY OF JESUS

The Book of Revelation concludes with a powerful reaffirmation of Jesus' eternal sovereignty and the promise of His imminent return. His words, "Surely I am coming quickly" (Revelation 22:20), offer hope and assurance to believers, emphasizing His ultimate authority and the fulfillment of God's divine purposes. By examining these verses through an expository study with exhaustive Strong's Concordance, we can uncover the profound meanings and significant truths revealed in this concluding chapter.

Jesus' Eternal Sovereignty

Revelation 22:6-7 highlights the faithfulness and truth of God's words and the blessedness of keeping them:

> "Then he said to me, 'These words are faithful and true.' And the Lord God of the holy prophets sent His angel to show His servants the things which must shortly take place. 'Behold, I am coming quickly! Blessed is he who keeps the words of the prophecy of this book.'"

- Faithful and True (πιστο□ ς και□ αληθινός - Strong's G4103, G228): Emphasizes the reliability and veracity of God's words.

- Lord God of the Holy Prophets (Κυ ριος Θεο ς ὁ ἅγιος προφη της - Strong's G2962, G2316, G40, G4396): Indicates the divine source of prophecy.

- Angel (α γγελος - Strong's G32): Represents a messenger of God.

- Shortly Take Place (τα χος γι νομαι - Strong's G5034, G1096): Indicates the imminence of the events described.

- Coming Quickly (ε ρχομαι ταχύ - Strong's G2064, G5035): Emphasizes the sudden and imminent return of Jesus.

- Blessed (μακα ριος - Strong's G3107): Indicates a state of happiness and favor.

- Keeps the Words (τηρε ω ὁ λο γος - Strong's G5083, G3588, G3056): Refers to obedience and adherence to the prophetic message.

Jesus' eternal sovereignty is underscored by the faithfulness and truth of His words and the assurance of His imminent return. The blessedness of keeping the words of the prophecy highlights the importance of obedience and readiness.

Worship and Admonition

Revelation 22:8-11 describes John's reaction and the angel's admonition:

> "Now I, John, saw and heard these things. And when I heard and saw, I fell down to worship before the feet of the angel who showed me these things. Then he said to me, 'See that you do not do that. For I am your fellow servant, and of your brethren the prophets, and of those who keep the words of this book. Worship God.' And he said to me, 'Do not seal the words of the prophecy of this book, for the time is at hand. He who is unjust, let him be unjust still; he who is filthy, let him be filthy still; he who is righteous, let him be righteous still; he who is holy, let him be holy still.'"

- John (Ἰωάννης - Strong's G2491): The author of Revelation.

- Worship (προσκυνε□ω - Strong's G4352): Indicates reverence and adoration.

- Fellow Servant (συ□νδουλος - Strong's G4889): Represents a co-worker in God's service.

- Prophets (προφη□της - Strong's G4396): Refers to those who speak forth God's message.

- Time is at Hand (καιρο□ς ἐγγὺς - Strong's G2540, G1451): Indicates the nearness of the fulfillment of prophecy.

- Unjust, Filthy, Righteous, Holy (α□δικος, ῥυπαρός, δίκαιος, ἅγιος - Strong's G94, G4508, G1342, G40): Describes the states of human character and behavior.

John's reaction to worship the angel and the subsequent admonition to worship God alone highlight the centrality of God in the prophetic vision. The instruction not to seal the words of the prophecy emphasizes the urgency and immediacy of the message.

The Imminent Return of Jesus

Revelation 22:12-17 emphasizes Jesus' imminent return and the call to righteousness:

> "'And behold, I am coming quickly, and My reward is with Me, to give to every one according to his work. I am the Alpha and the Omega, the Beginning and the End, the First and the Last.' Blessed are those who do His commandments, that they may have the right to the tree of life, and may enter through the gates into the city. But outside are dogs and sorcerers and sexually immoral and murderers and idolaters, and whoever loves and practices a lie. I, Jesus, have sent My angel to testify to you these things in the churches. I am the Root and the Offspring of David, the Bright and Morning Star. And the Spirit and the bride say, 'Come!' And let him who hears say, 'Come!' And let him who thirsts come. Whoever desires, let him take the water of life freely.'"

- Coming Quickly (ἔρχομαι ταχύ - Strong's G2064, G5035): Emphasizes the sudden and imminent return of Jesus.

- Reward (μισθός - Strong's G3408): Represents recompense for deeds.

- Alpha and Omega (Ἄλφα καὶ Ὠμέγα - Strong's G1, G5598): Represents Jesus as the beginning and the end.

- Tree of Life (ξύλον ζωῆ - Strong's G3586, G2222): Symbolizes eternal life.

- Gates into the City (πυλών εἰς ἡ πόλις - Strong's G4440, G1519, G3588, G4172): Represents entry into the New Jerusalem.

- Dogs, Sorcerers, Immoral, Murderers, Idolaters (κύων, φάρμακος, πόρνος, φονεύς, εἰδωλολάτρης - Strong's G2965, G5332, G4205, G5406, G1496): Describes those excluded from the kingdom.

- Root and Offspring of David (ῥίζα καὶ γένος Δαυίδ - Strong's G4491, G1085, G1138): Indicates Jesus' messianic lineage.

- Bright and Morning Star (λαμπρός καὶ πρωϊνός ἀστήρ - Strong's G2986, G3720, G792): Symbolizes Jesus' glory and guidance.

- Spirit and the Bride (πνεῦμα καὶ ἡ νύμφη - Strong's G4151, G2532, G3588, G3565): Represents the call of the Holy Spirit and the Church.

- Water of Life (ὑδωρ ζωή - Strong's G5204, G2222): Symbolizes the gift of eternal life.

Jesus' imminent return and the promise of reward emphasize the urgency of living righteously. The invitation to take the water of life freely highlights the grace and inclusivity of the gospel.

The Warning and the Promise

Revelation 22:18-20 provides a solemn warning and a reaffirmation of Jesus' return:

> "For I testify to everyone who hears the words of the prophecy of this book: If anyone adds to these things, God will add to him the plagues that are written in this book; and if anyone takes away from the words of the book of this prophecy, God shall take away his part from the Book of Life, from the holy city, and from the things which are written in this book. He who testifies to these things says, 'Surely I am coming quickly.' Amen. Even so, come, Lord Jesus!"

- Testify (μαρτυρέω - Strong's G3140): Indicates solemn affirmation.

- Adds, Takes Away (προστίθημι, ἀφαιρέω - Strong's G4369, G851): Represents altering the prophetic message.

- Plagues (πληγη□ - Strong's G4127): Refers to divine judgments.

- Book of Life (βι□βλος ζωη□ - Strong's G976, G2222): Symbolizes the record of those who belong to Christ.

- Holy City (ἁ□ γιος πο□ λις - Strong's G40, G4172): Represents the New Jerusalem.

- Coming Quickly (ε□ ρχομαι ταχύ - Strong's G2064, G5035): Emphasizes the imminent return of Jesus.

The warning against altering the prophetic message underscores the sanctity and authority of God's word. The reaffirmation of Jesus' imminent return provides hope and anticipation for believers.

Benediction

Revelation 22:21 concludes with a benediction:

> "The grace of our Lord Jesus Christ be with you all. Amen."

- Grace (χα□ ρις - Strong's G5485): Represents divine favor and blessing.

- Lord Jesus Christ (Κυ□ ριος Ἰησοῦς Χριστός - Strong's G2962, G2424, G5547): Affirms the divinity and lordship of Jesus.

The benediction emphasizes the grace and favor of Jesus Christ, providing a fitting conclusion to the profound and hopeful message of Revelation.

Expository Insights

Examining the text through exhaustive Strong's Concordance reveals deeper meanings and connections:

- πιστο□ς και□ αληθινός (Strong's G4103, G228): Emphasizes the reliability and veracity of God's words.

- Κυ□ριος Θεο□ς ὁ ἅγιος προφη□της (Strong's G2962, G2316, G40, G4396): Indicates the divine source of prophecy.

- α□γγελος (Strong's G32): Represents a messenger of God.

- τα□χος γι□νομαι (Strong's G5034, G1096): Indicates the imminence of the events described.

- ε□ρχομαι ταχύ (Strong's G2064, G5035): Emphasizes the sudden and imminent return of Jesus.

- μακα□ριος (Strong's G3107): Indicates a state of happiness and favor.

- τηρε□ω ὁ λο□γος (Strong's G5083, G3588, G3056): Refers to obedience and adherence to the prophetic message.

- Ἰωάννης (Strong's G2491): The author of Revelation.

- προσκυνε□ω (Strong's G4352): Indicates reverence and adoration.

- συ□νδουλος (Strong's G4889): Represents a co-worker in God's service.

- προφη□της (Strong's G4396): Refers to those who speak forth God's message.

- καιρο□ς ἐγγύς (Strong's G2540, G1451): Indicates the nearness of the fulfillment of prophecy.

- α□δικος, ῥυπαρός, δίκαιος, ἅγιος (Strong's G94, G4508, G1342, G40): Describes the states of human character and behavior.

- μισθο□ς (Strong's G3408): Represents recompense for deeds.

- ξυ□λον ζωη□ (Strong's G3586, G2222): Symbolizes eternal life.

- πυλω□ν εἰς ἡ πόλις (Strong's G4440, G1519, G3588, G4172): Represents entry into the New Jerusalem.

- κυ□ων, φάρμακος, πόρνος, φονεύς, εἰδωλολάτρης (Strong's G2965, G5332, G4205, G5406, G1496): Describes those excluded from the kingdom.

- ῥίζα και□ γένος Δαυίδ (Strong's G4491, G1085, G1138): Indicates Jesus' messianic lineage.

- λαμπρο□ς και□ πρωϊνός ἀστήρ (Strong's G2986, G3720, G792): Symbolizes Jesus' glory and guidance.

- πνεῦμα και□ ἡ νύμφη (Strong's G4151, G2532, G3588, G3565): Represents the call of the Holy Spirit and the Church.

- ὑ□δωρ ζωή (Strong's G5204, G2222): Symbolizes the gift of eternal life.

- μαρτυρε□ω (Strong's G3140): Indicates solemn affirmation.

- προστι□θημι, ἀφαιρέω (Strong's G4369, G851): Represents altering the prophetic message.

- πληγη□ (Strong's G4127): Refers to divine judgments.

- βι□βλος ζωη□ (Strong's G976, G2222): Symbolizes the record of those who belong to Christ.

- ἁ□γιος πο□λις (Strong's G40, G4172): Represents the New Jerusalem.

- χα□ρις (Strong's G5485): Represents divine favor and blessing.

- Κυ□ριος Ἰησοῦς Χριστός (Strong's G2962, G2424, G5547): Affirms the divinity and lordship of Jesus.

Practical Application

The conclusion of Revelation emphasizes the eternal sovereignty of Jesus and holds timeless relevance for believers today. Key lessons include:

1. Recognizing Jesus' Authority: The reaffirmation of Jesus' sovereignty emphasizes His ultimate authority and power to execute judgment and fulfill God's purposes. Believers are called to recognize and submit to His lordship.

2. Living in Anticipation of Jesus' Return: The repeated emphasis on Jesus' imminent return encourages believers to live in readiness, maintaining faithfulness and obedience.

3. Embracing the Prophetic Message: The admonition to keep the words of the prophecy and the warning against altering it highlight the importance of adhering to God's word with reverence and integrity.

4. Finding Assurance in God's Promise: The promise of reward and the invitation to take the water of life freely provide assurance of God's grace and the hope of eternal life.

5. Living as Faithful Witnesses: The call to righteousness and the example of the prophets and servants of God encourage believers to live as faithful witnesses, proclaiming the truth and standing firm in their faith.

Conclusion

The conclusion of the Book of Revelation provides a profound reaffirmation of Jesus' eternal sovereignty and the promise of His imminent return. Through the imagery of the great white throne, the warnings and promises, and the benediction of grace, believers are called to recognize Jesus' authority, live in anticipation of His return, embrace the prophetic message, find assurance in God's promise, and live as faithful witnesses. By examining these verses through an expository study with exhaustive Strong's Concordance, we uncover the depth of this vision and its enduring relevance for the church today. As we embrace the truths revealed in the eternal sovereignty of Jesus, we will be drawn into deeper worship and greater readiness to stand firm in our faith, eagerly awaiting the fulfillment of God's divine purposes.

FINAL THOUGHTS BY DR. MAXWELL SHIMBA

The Book of Revelation stands as a testament to the divinity and sovereignty of Jesus Christ, offering profound insights into His ultimate authority and eternal reign. As the Alpha and Omega, Jesus encapsulates the beginning and the end, asserting His control over all creation and the unfolding of God's divine plan. This prophetic book, rich with visions and judgments, not only foretells the ultimate victory over evil but also provides a beacon of hope and assurance for believers.

The vivid imagery and powerful declarations within Revelation highlight key aspects of Jesus' nature and mission. His depiction as the victorious warrior, the righteous judge, and the eternal King serves to reinforce His central role in God's redemptive plan. Each vision, from the binding of Satan to the establishment of the new heaven and new earth, underscores the triumph of righteousness and the final eradication of sin and suffering.

Jesus' words, "Behold, I make all things new," resonate with a promise of renewal and restoration. This promise extends beyond the apocalyptic events described, reaching into the hearts of believers, calling them to a life of faithfulness and anticipation of His return. The prophetic messages to the seven churches, the unfolding of the seals, trumpets, and bowls, and the ultimate establishment of the New Jerusalem collectively paint a picture of a divine narrative that culminates in the eternal reign of Christ.

As we navigate the complexities and challenges of our world, the Book of Revelation provides a framework for understanding the cosmic battle between good and evil and the assurance of God's ultimate victory. It calls us to steadfastness, to remain faithful in the face of trials, and to live in the light of Jesus' imminent return.

In embracing the lessons of Revelation, we are reminded of the certainty of Jesus' triumph and the hope of His coming kingdom. His sovereignty guarantees that justice will prevail, that every tear will be wiped away, and that eternal joy will replace the sorrows of this world. As believers, we are called to hold fast to these truths, to let them shape our lives and our faith, and to eagerly await the fulfillment of all things in Christ.

May the study of Revelation deepen our understanding of Jesus' divine sovereignty, strengthen our faith in His promises, and inspire us to live as faithful witnesses to His glory. Even so, come, Lord Jesus!

Dr. Maxwell Shimba

APPENDICES

Appendix A: Key Greek Terms in Revelation

Understanding the original Greek terms used in the Book of Revelation can provide deeper insights into its meaning and theological significance. Here is a list of key Greek terms frequently encountered in the text, along with their Strong's Concordance numbers and brief explanations:

1. Alpha and Omega (Αλφα καιⲯ Ωμέγα - Strong's G1, G5598): Represents Jesus as the beginning and the end, emphasizing His eternal nature and sovereignty.

2. Faithful and True (πιστοⲯ ς καιⲯ αληθινός - Strong's G4103, G228): Describes Jesus' reliability and trustworthiness in executing judgment and fulfilling promises.

3. Lamb (αμνός - Strong's G721): Symbolizes Jesus as the sacrificial Lamb who redeems humanity through His death and resurrection.

4. Witness (μαρτυριⲯ α - Strong's G3141): Refers to the testimony of Jesus, highlighting His role as the faithful witness to God's truth.

5. Throne (θρο□νος - Strong's G2362): Represents the seat of divine authority and judgment, frequently associated with God's sovereignty and Jesus' reign.

6. Book of Life (βι□βλος ζωη□ - Strong's G976, G2222): Symbolizes the record of those who belong to Christ and are granted eternal life.

7. New Jerusalem (καινο□ς Ἱερουσαλήμ - Strong's G2537, G2419): Represents the ultimate dwelling place of God with His people, symbolizing the fulfillment of God's redemptive plan.

8. Overcome (νικα□ω - Strong's G3528): Describes the victory of believers who remain faithful to Jesus amidst trials and persecution.

9. Holy (ἅγιος - Strong's G40): Refers to the sanctity and purity of God, His people, and the New Jerusalem.

10. Judgment (κρι□σις - Strong's G2920): Indicates the act of divine judgment executed by Jesus, reflecting His righteousness and justice.

Appendix B: Major Themes in Revelation

Revelation is rich with themes that convey the theological and eschatological messages of the text. Here are some major themes explored in the book:

1. Jesus' Sovereignty: Revelation repeatedly emphasizes Jesus' authority as the Alpha and Omega, the beginning and the end, and the ruler over all creation. His sovereignty is depicted through various visions and titles, affirming His ultimate control over the unfolding of history.

2. Divine Judgment: The book contains numerous scenes of divine judgment, including the opening of the seven seals, the sounding of the seven trumpets, and the pouring out of the seven bowls of wrath. These judgments highlight God's righteousness and the inevitability of divine justice.

3. Victory Over Evil: Revelation portrays the ultimate triumph of Jesus over the forces of evil, including Satan, the beast, and the false prophet. This theme underscores the certainty of God's victory and the defeat of all opposition to His reign.

4. Hope and Encouragement: The prophetic visions offer hope and encouragement to believers, assuring them of God's faithfulness and the fulfillment of His promises. The depiction of the new heaven and new earth, the New Jerusalem, and the river of life provides a vision of eternal joy and peace.

5. Call to Faithfulness: The messages to the seven churches in chapters 2 and 3 emphasize the need for believers to remain faithful and steadfast in their faith. These messages

address various challenges and encourage perseverance amidst persecution and trials.

6. Eschatological Fulfillment: Revelation depicts the ultimate fulfillment of God's redemptive plan, including the final judgment, the eradication of sin and suffering, and the establishment of God's eternal kingdom. This theme underscores the eschatological hope that believers hold.

Appendix C: Symbols and Imagery in Revelation

Revelation is renowned for its symbolic and often enigmatic imagery. Here are some of the key symbols and their interpretations:

1. Seven: Represents completeness and perfection. Examples include the seven churches, seven seals, seven trumpets, and seven bowls.

2. Beast (θηρι ον - Strong's G2342): Symbolizes oppressive and blasphemous political power, often associated with the Antichrist.

3. Dragon (δρα κων - Strong's G1404): Represents Satan, the ancient serpent and adversary of God and His people.

4. White Horse (λευκο ς ππος - Strong's G3022, G2462): Symbolizes victory and purity, often associated with Jesus as the conquering King.

5. Babylon (Βαβυλων - Strong's G897): Represents the corrupt and idolatrous systems of the world, often depicted as a great harlot.

6. New Jerusalem: Symbolizes the ultimate dwelling place of God with His people, representing the fulfillment of God's redemptive plan and the eternal state of believers.

7. Lamb (ἀμνός): Represents Jesus as the sacrificial Lamb who redeems humanity through His death and resurrection.

8. Seal (σφραγιζω - Strong's G4972): Symbolizes security and ownership, often associated with God's protection of His people.

9. Mark of the Beast (χαραγμα θηριον - Strong's G5480, G2342): Represents allegiance to the Antichrist and opposition to God.

10. Tree of Life (ξυλον ζωη - Strong's G3586, G2222): Symbolizes eternal life and the restoration of paradise.

Appendix D: Chronology of Events in Revelation

Understanding the chronological sequence of events in Revelation can help readers grasp the overall narrative and prophetic timeline:

1. Introduction and Vision of the Glorified Christ (Revelation 1): John receives the initial vision of Jesus and is instructed to write to the seven churches.

2. Messages to the Seven Churches (Revelation 2-3): Jesus addresses each of the seven churches with specific commendations, warnings, and promises.

3. Heavenly Throne Room Vision (Revelation 4-5): John is taken to the throne room of God, where he witnesses the worship of the Lamb who is worthy to open the scroll.

4. Opening of the Seven Seals (Revelation 6-8): Each seal reveals a specific judgment or event, culminating in the opening of the seventh seal and the silence in heaven.

5. Sounding of the Seven Trumpets (Revelation 8-11): Each trumpet brings a new judgment upon the earth, leading to the final trumpet that heralds the kingdom of God.

6. Conflict Between the Woman and the Dragon (Revelation 12): The cosmic battle between God's people and Satan is depicted, emphasizing Jesus' victory.

7. Rise of the Beasts and the False Prophet (Revelation 13): The Antichrist and the false prophet deceive and persecute the faithful.

8. Visions of Judgment and Harvest (Revelation 14-15): The final judgments are prepared, and the harvest of the earth is reaped.

9. Pouring Out of the Seven Bowls of Wrath (Revelation 16): God's wrath is poured out in full measure upon the earth.

10. Fall of Babylon (Revelation 17-18): The judgment and destruction of the corrupt world system symbolized by Babylon.

11. Triumphant Return of Christ (Revelation 19): Jesus returns as the victorious warrior, defeating the beast and the false prophet.

12. Millennium and Final Judgment (Revelation 20): Satan is bound for a thousand years, followed by the final judgment before the great white throne.

13. New Heaven and New Earth (Revelation 21-22): The ultimate fulfillment of God's redemptive plan with the establishment of the new heaven and new earth and the eternal reign of Jesus.

Appendix E: Practical Applications for Believers

Revelation provides numerous lessons and practical applications for believers today. Here are some key takeaways:

1. Remain Faithful: The messages to the seven churches encourage believers to remain steadfast in their faith, despite trials and persecution. Maintaining a strong relationship with Jesus and living according to His teachings is essential.

2. Anticipate Jesus' Return: The repeated emphasis on Jesus' imminent return calls believers to live in readiness, keeping their lives aligned with God's will and looking forward to His coming kingdom.

3. Trust in God's Justice: The visions of divine judgment reassure believers that God will ultimately bring justice and righteousness. This trust can provide comfort and strength in the face of injustice and suffering.

4. Embrace Hope: The depiction of the new heaven and new earth offers a vision of eternal joy and peace. Believers can find hope and encouragement in the promise of eternal life and the ultimate restoration of all things.

5. Witness Boldly: Revelation challenges believers to be faithful witnesses, proclaiming the truth of the gospel and standing firm in their testimony of Jesus.

6. Live Righteously: The call to holiness and righteousness throughout Revelation encourages believers to live lives that reflect God's character and values, avoiding the corrupt practices of the world.

Appendix F: Further Reading and Resources

For those interested in further study of Revelation and its themes, here are some recommended resources:

1. "The Revelation

of John" by William Barclay: A comprehensive commentary on the Book of Revelation, offering historical and theological insights.

2. "Revelation: Four Views, A Parallel Commentary" by Steve Gregg: Presents four different interpretations of Revelation, providing a broad perspective on its meaning.

3. "The Message of Revelation" by Michael Wilcock: A thoughtful and accessible commentary that explores the themes and messages of Revelation.

4. "The Book of Revelation: A Commentary on the Greek Text" by G. K. Beale: A detailed and scholarly commentary focusing on the original Greek text.

5. "Revelation: An Introduction and Commentary" by Leon Morris: An introductory commentary that provides a clear and concise explanation of Revelation's key themes and messages.

These resources can enhance your understanding and provide additional perspectives on the rich and complex messages of the Book of Revelation.